Finding Grace & Peace

IN SPITE OF

Trials & Tragedy

John & Joann Ashley

All Scripture quotations are taken from the
King James Version

First Edition
Copyright 2016 by The Bible Nation Society

The Bible Nation Society
2680 E. M-21
Corunna, MI 48817
989.720.2267

Layout by Jordan Napier
Design by Josh Levesque

ISBN-13: 978-0998480404
ISBN-10: 0998480401

BISAC: Religion / Christian Life / Inspirational

Contents

Foreward

Pastor Steven G. Brown

I would like to invite you to settle in and read this wonderful book that is written by my dear friend, Pastor John Ashley. He will tell you his story about how the Lord gifted him and his dear wife, Joann, with a very special son, Johnny. Their older sons, Bob and Jason, are also a large part in this family's story. With refreshing candidness, John will take you on a journey with his family through the many fears, joys, sorrows, laughter, sadness, and strength needed to face the challenges of caring for a child who has severe physical and emotional needs. Caregivers that face many of the same challenges will find this book a source of encouragement.

I have had the privilege of knowing the Ashley family for many years and have found them to be one of the sweetest families I have known throughout my 36 years of ministry. Over this time, I have observed, firsthand, many of the trials, as well as, the victories that John, Joann, Johnny and his brothers have faced. I will say, without reservation, that the Ashley family, with the help of their Heavenly Father, has "come forth as gold."

It has been an honor to for me to write the foreword for this book. As you get a glimpse into the lives of each member of this

In Spite Of

precious family, that was chosen of God for His unique purpose, I trust that you will be blessed and your faith increased in the One who knows our every care.

Pastor Steven G. Brown
Senior Pastor of Parkview Baptist Church, Livonia, Michigan

Acknowledgments

This book has been a labor of love and has been written with a wide range of emotions. This work could never have been done without the help and support of many people close to Joann and me.

First of all, I would like to thank our sons, Bob and Jason. Your mom and I have been blessed to have you in our lives; Johnny loved you both so much. Your help in raising Johnny was priceless and your contribution to making this book possible is much appreciated. I would also like to thank their wives, Rebekah and Kristin for their help with the proof reading and editing of this work.

There are many others to whom I want to express a sincere thanks for being a great help to this project: Pastor Steve Brown and his wife, Pam, for their support and love; Bob and Linda Tedrick, for their feedback and friendship; Sandy Helzerman, for her editing and correcting my English; Caleb Jenkins, for his honest assessment; Sarah Bowling, for all the work she did in editing and reviewing; Linda Stumpo, for her corrections and honesty; Becky Calaman, for ensuring a proper approach to speaking of Johnny's deafness; Lisa Mininni, for the encouragement she has been to see this project through; Pastor Jason Georges, for encouraging me to finally sit

In Spite Of

down and write this book; Pastor Josh Levesque, for all the work he has done and putting up with my many delays; and Jordan Napier, for doing all the formatting work that needed to be done. I also want to thank the countless others who have encouraged us to take on the work of writing this book.

I want to thank my co-author wife of over forty years, Joann, for the work she put into this book. We wrote this book through many tears and it has proven to be great therapy for us. Thank you, Joann, for putting up with my impatience. I love you.

Lastly, and most importantly, I want to thank the Lord Jesus Christ for the motivation to write this book, and the grace and strength that He has provided in our lives through the years of trials and triumphs. Without His intervention in our lives we would have never been privileged to have a relationship with God and to have had Johnny in our family.

Introduction

This book is about a family's journey of faith through twenty eight-years of caregiving. The title "In Spite of" is how our son Johnny lived his life. Despite the many challenges he faced, he was an inspiration to all who knew him. "In Spite of" caring for Johnny, our family was able to serve God by the strength and power that He gave to us all.

Much of Johnny's medical history is recorded in this book although, it is not in a chronological order. Johnny came into this world with multiple congenital malformations. He endured over forty surgeries including; two heart valve replacements and a kidney transplant. At the age of two and a half we discovered Johnny was also profoundly deaf. At the time of his birth the tests were not available to check for Deafness like they are today and with so many other issues we never considered the possibility that he was deaf.

Although this book details many of the struggles and victories our family experienced during our years of caring for Johnny, it has as its main character the One who sustained us through the journey and that is our Lord and Savior Jesus Christ. Without His ever-abiding presence in our lives, we would have lost all hope and, most likely, given up on Johnny and each other.

In Spite Of

Years ago, as I listened to a talk show on the radio on my drive home from work, the host was speaking to a young man that was struggling with the birth of his child with disabilities. I couldn't help but call and get involved in the conversation. I tried to give some advice to the young man and those who knew this couple. The host quickly turned the conversation to talk about the situation with our son. He asked me sort of a leading question; "What is it that you have learned about yourself through your experience?" (At that time Johnny was only about seven years old). I quickly responded, "I learned how much I need the Lord's power and strength to sustain me through our trials". Well, not being satisfied with my answer, he rephrased the question. "Yes, but, what is it that you most learned about yourself through this all?" I could only respond by saying, "I learned that I need the Lord every day, and without Him I would never be able to handle the challenges that we have faced."

I knew the answer that the host had in mind was, "I learned that I can handle more than I ever thought I could." That thought has never entered my mind. I knew I couldn't handle this. Jesus put it best in John 15:5, "*I am the vine, ye are the branches: he that abideth in me, and I in him, the same bringeth forth much fruit: for without me ye can do nothing.*"

Through the years of caring for Johnny, our family has endeavored to keep the Lord first in our lives. At times I know that we (or should I say I) have failed at that, but, by God's grace we have mostly trusted Johnny to His care.

It is our desire that this book will be a help and a blessing to all who read it, especially to those unsung heroes that care for one of God's creations. Those that, "In Spite of" the stress, the pressure, the heartache, and the frustrations that come from being a caregiver, live their lives to the best of their abilities. People that are not medical professionals, yet are far too familiar with medical terminology that relates to those they may care for.

All of us have an "In Spite of" in our lives. Each trial and problem that we face can be used as an excuse or a catalyst for our lives. If we choose to use it as an excuse, we could find ourselves many times sad, lonely and stuck. However, if we see our "In Spite of" situations as a motivation to help others we can become an inspiration and an encourager to many people.

We also pray that this book will encourage those that know a caregiver. May you learn to open your heart and allow them to have a platform to speak, to vent, and to know someone is there for them to just listen.

Thank you for taking time to read this book. You may not gain any great insights or profound truths you don't presently know, but, my prayer is that, you will understand the strength that can only come from a loving caring Savior and realize that we can live extraordinary lives "In Spite of" our trials.

John and Joann Ashley

Chapter One

In Spite of Our Prayers

Proverbs 27:1 "Boast not thyself of to morrow; for thou knowest not what a day may bring forth."

It was unusually warm for the end of April in Michigan with the temperature in the low 80s. Everyone was so happy to have such nice weather after a long winter, but the excitement of warm weather was nothing compared to the anticipation of our baby's arrival. This was going to be the little girl for whom we had prayed for more than a year. We just knew that God was about to answer that prayer.

You see it was about a year and a half before that a radical change had taken place in our family. We had two wonderful boys, and life was just going along just fine when Joann felt there was something missing in our marriage and some changes needed to be made. That was when a close friend of hers invited her to go and visit a young lady that she knew. Little did Joann know that this encounter was directed by the Lord Himself.

When they met, this young lady kept talking about God as if she knew Him personally. This piqued Joann's interest. After all, she was religious enough. She went to church with the kids from time to time, but having a personal relationship with the Lord was something she didn't know was a possibility. At the end of the evening this young lady handed Joann a book on the family and said, "You might enjoy this .

As she read the book, it spoke to her heart, not just about our family issues, but also about how to have a personal relationship with God through Jesus Christ. The book explained how we are all estranged from God because of our sin and that through Jesus Christ's sacrifice on the cross we could be forgiven, and have eternal life, and possess that personal relationship with God she desired. It was then that she realized her own personal need for forgiveness. She asked God to forgive her of her sins and received Christ as her Savior. Peace came in and flooded her soul! With new found joy she came and talked to me about this personal relationship with Jesus.

I was at a completely different stage in my life at that time. I thought things were good and wasn't concerned much about our family issues. As a matter of fact, I was just cruising through life, living for myself, and didn't care about much else. I was having fun partying with my friends and outwardly was having a blast in life! But there was a secret that no one really knew, I was miserable inside.

Outwardly I had no religious affiliations; I mean I rarely went to church. I would send Joann and the boys off to church and I would sleep off Saturday nights while they were gone. But, inwardly, God was working me over. You see ten years earlier, while in the Navy and stationed in Pensacola, Florida, I started that personal relationship with God myself. It happened one night while I was in the barracks washing clothes. A good friend of mine came up to me and began talking about Jesus with me. I realized that I knew nothing about Him apart from Christmas and Easter.

My friend knew very little himself, but contacted an officer who came and explained the same message of God's forgiveness that Joann would hear years later. It was at that point I bowed my heart and will to God and trusted Christ as my Savior. Suddenly my life began to change. Instead of being in constant trouble, I began conforming to the standards the Navy had for me which made my life a lot easier. I found a joy and peace that can only come from God.

Well, as time passed, I slowly got away from the Lord, but He never left me. I went back to the world the he had brought me out of and in an attempt to quiet the battle raging inside me, I turned to all the world could bring. That was when Joann and I got married; high school sweethearts were now husband and wife. She had known of my conversion to Christ but never really saw a change in my life and thought it was a passing thing for me. For nine years, there was turmoil going on in my heart that manifested itself in anger and a self-centered life.

When Joann came to me and told me that she desired to have a family like the one the book she was reading talked about, it was like God shot an arrow into my heart. I could almost hear Him say to me, "This is your last chance to get in right relationship with me." I told Joann we would begin going to church that Sunday. Well, by God's grace we haven't stopped going since.

So you see, the prayer that we were sure God was about to answer came from a couple that the Lord had radically changed. We were now a Christian home and were busy serving and being faithful to Him and our church. We really wanted that girl. One of my wife's good friends even bought a frilly pink dress for our baby girl to wear.

So on that warm April day, we headed off to the hospital to have our new baby girl delivered. There was no rush, no labor pains because she was to be delivered by caesarian-section on May 1st. The maternity area was recently remodeled and was beautiful. This

In Spite Of

delivery would be the first that I would be able to take part in. Our oldest son, Bob, was an emergency C-section and I was not allowed in the delivery room. Our second born, Jason, was a scheduled C-section and they weren't allowing people to be with the mother during the procedure. This time, however, I was in! They were allowing the fathers to be in the delivery room during the operation. Armed with our relatively new faith and a deep love for each other, we entered the delivery room ready for whatever God had in store for us. Or so we thought.

The delivery room was a sea of green sheets to me. They sat me next to Joann's head, with the sheets creating a barrier between us and the doctors and nurses. Everyone was in a cheerful mood and ready to bring this new life into the world. The delivery team were all busy working away as I stared at Joann and thanked God in my heart for giving me a wonderful wife and giving us a new baby. I remember silently praying in my heart for things to go well with the delivery. I was splitting my time between looking at Joann and watching the doctor as he delivered the baby.

Then he said, "It's a boy." I remember a feeling of disappointment and wondering how Joann was feeling. I found it strange that the doctor and the nurse that was aiding him kept looking at each other. Then the doctor said, "He has a hair-lip. Do you know what that is?" Joann said, "I think so." Then the delivery team all began to reassure us "They can work wonders with surgery nowadays and you won't even be able to tell".

Suddenly, the nurse came and brought our son to us. He had a huge hole in his face! His tongue was sticking out at us. He had no nostrils in his nose, just a huge hole. His skin was white, and his eyes were pointing in two different directions. What? This can't be the baby we had prayed for! Joann immediately began to cry. They quickly took Johnny away to Neo-Natal Intensive Care. Johnny... We were so certain that he was going to be a girl, that we really hadn't spent much time discussing boy's names, so we just decided to name him John, after his dad. We always called him Johnny.

The verse that is quoted at the beginning of this chapter was kind of adopted by us as our "family verse", if you will. Life has a way of taking sudden turns in completely different directions than those we plan. From joy and excitement of having a baby girl, we were cast into the shock and grief of having a child with special needs. Little did we know that over the next several years this verse would be proven to be so very meaningful in our lives.

I was escorted from the delivery room to a locker room to change out of my scrubs and then go to the waiting room where the doctor would come and speak with me. I didn't want to leave Joann alone, but I couldn't stay in the delivery room while they finished the procedure. They could take care of her physical needs, but who would care for her emotionally and spiritually? I remember leaning on the lockers crying, wondering what was I going to do? Would our son graduate from high school? Would he have a girlfriend? Then the realization hit me, "I can't handle this." In tears I remember crying out to the Lord and asking Him for His grace and strength, admitting to Him that "I'm not strong enough to deal with what lies ahead."

Once I had changed, I sat anxiously in the waiting area until the doctor came to talk with me. It seemed as though everyone was staring at me. It was no wonder, I was sitting in shock, with tear-filled eyes staring into space. The doctor finally came in and assured me that Joann was fine and in recovery, and that the baby was stable and in the Intensive Care unit. He said my wife would be in recovery for a while and a nurse would come and get me in a couple of hours to let me know when I could see her. "Oh yes", I thought, "I need to see Joann, to try to comfort her to hold her and tell her that I love her. She is going to need me." Then I thought; "What could I possibly say to her that would comfort her? Man, this is going to be rough."

In Spite Of

I thought about the phone calls that needed to be made. People were waiting to hear the news. The first call I had to make was to Joann's Mom. How is she going to take this? I vaguely remember making those calls; I was just doing what had to be done. I was fighting back tears with each word getting stuck in my throat, "It's a boy, but he has some problems. He has a cleft-lip and palate, and he seems to have some other issues that will be looked into. Joann is fine and I will see her soon." (Joann's parents were taking care of our other two boys while we were at the hospital.) Next, I called my Mom and then I called the church to ask them to pray for us and our son.

After the phone calls, I went back to the waiting room to find out when I could see my wife. It was going to be a while, so I sat and stared and thought, and cried. Then, like an angel of mercy, my sister Jenny showed up. "Thank the Lord, someone to talk to." She sat and cried with me for a while and then asked, "Have you gone and seen the baby yet?" That question hit me like a ton of bricks. I was so worried about Joann, myself, and how I was going to deal with this, that I hadn't thought about going and seeing him. Jenny said she would wait there for me, but I should go and see my son. She was so right; that was exactly what I needed to do.

Neo-Natal Intensive Care is a busy place with nurses and doctors moving about, monitoring every incubator, monitors beeping and babies crying. In order for me to see Johnny, I had to put on a gown and wear a mask over my mouth and nose. Seeing him for the first time in I.C.U. was a little overwhelming. At that time, I was still pretty much numb and all the information that the medical staff was giving me was kind of wasted on me right then. Shock had set in and I was barely coherent. It was far too much to be digested at one time, but there was no doubt in my mind that our newborn son would need a lot of care as time went on.

The nurse directed me to John's incubator and asked; "Would

you like to hold him?" I said that I would, even though I was so fearful inside. Although he was different and not that beautiful little girl we had imagined, he was my son, the child that God had given to us. As I held this helpless baby in my arms for the first time, the tears flowed freely. I rocked him in the chair the nurse brought over and hummed the song we had been singing to him since Joann became pregnant, "Jesus loves me this I know, for the Bible tells me so…" I prayed, "Lord, I know you love this special child, and Joann and me. Would you please send us your comfort at this time."

After a brief time with Johnny, I headed back to the waiting room where my sister was sitting. Joann was still in recovery and they didn't want me back with her yet. I told my sister all that I knew about the baby's condition and she stayed with me until they called me back to see my wife. To this day I am so grateful for my sister's visit that day. She was exactly what I needed to get me through those first couple of hours.

Finally, they called me back to the recovery area to see Joann. She was covered in a warm blanket up to her neck. She looked comfortable, but she started crying as I made eye contact with her. No words were said at first, we just wept together. I finally asked her how she felt. (What a stupid question) I wanted to know how she was doing physically, but she, like me, was numb from the shock we had just experienced. Joann finally spoke and I will never forget her words; "How can something that hurts so bad be good?" She was referencing a familiar passage of Scripture Romans 8:28 " *And we know that all things work together for good to them that love God, to them who are the called according to his purpose.*" For the first time, in what would be an endless list of questions concerning Johnny, I had no answer.

The next day we were still in shock. All we had prayed for and had hoped for was dashed. The best way I can describe it is that it was like someone took a shotgun, put it to my stomach and pulled

In Spite Of

the trigger. Joann was still recovering from the delivery, and from the grief over the loss of all that could have been. What made matters worse was seeing Joann's roommate with her healthy little girl doing what new mothers do, bonding with her new baby.

As we sat silently in the hospital room, I looked at her and said, "Honey he is our son; you need to go and see him." As hard as it would be, she agreed and we got her up and into a wheelchair and headed for the neo-natal intensive care unit.

When we arrived at Johnny's incubator there was an elderly nun standing next to him and talking to him. When Joann got to her feet to see Johnny the nun turned and said; "Are you his Mother? He is so sweet, and just think God chose you to be his mother." To my wife, this petite nun was the angel God sent to minister to her. That sweet lady reassured Joann that God had blessed her with this special child and that he had such a sweet personality. At the time Joann thought, "How could she know that?" However, that nun's words were prophetic. We certainly have been blessed. Johnny had the sweetest personality of anyone we know.

Our lives often take sudden and unexpected turns. We sometimes are confronted with drastic changes that we are personally unprepared for. All our plans for the future come crashing down around us and we need to reset our thinking. One thing that we can be sure of is that these sudden course corrections don't catch our Heavenly Father by surprise. Whatever has happened has first passed through his hands. Eventually we will see Romans 8:28 as a reality and not just a hopeful thought.

In Spite of Our Prayers

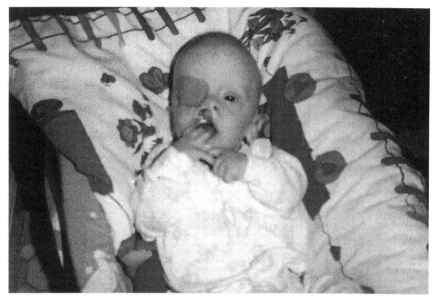

Johnny at 4mo. old. Eye patch to improve wall eyed

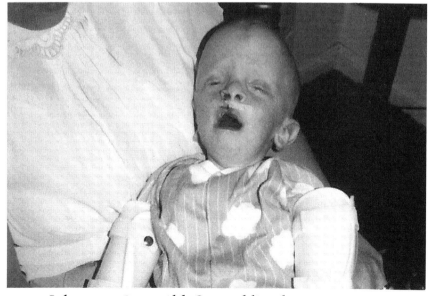

Johnny at 9mo. old. Second lip closure surgery

Jason at 5yrs. Johnny at 4mo. Bobby at 8yrs.

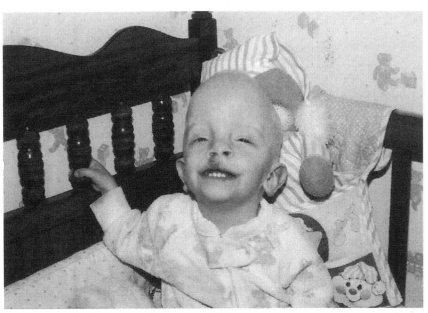

Johnny at 22mo.

Chapter Two

WHY? In Spite of Our Faith

Job 3:26 *"I was not in safety, neither had I rest, neither was I quiet; yet trouble came."*

Joann was discharged from the hospital a few days after Johnny entered into our lives, but he had to stay in I.C.U. for several more days. So began the daily trips to the hospital for Joann and me. Little did we know at the time, trips to the hospital would become an all too familiar task over the next twenty-eight years.

Though we didn't talk much about our personal feelings during those first few days, we both knew the internal struggle that was going on inside each other. As relatively new Christians, we couldn't understand the "WHY" of it all and unfortunately there were no satisfactory answers to that question. Many try to spiritualize the "WHY" questions: "For the glory of God"; "All things work together for good"; "The Lord knows what he's doing". These are all truths from the Word of God, but they can't relieve the heartache. The words just fall short of giving real answers to a question that only time and eternity will be able to answer.

In Spite Of

Our family had just started attending church regularly about a year and a half before Johnny was born and had really "jumped in". We attended all the services we could, soaking up the preaching and teaching of the Bible. And were busy serving in different capacities. I was a Sunday School teacher (learning as I went), bus driver, and involved in the prison ministry of our church. Joann was involved with the Ladies Bible Study and learning her role as godly wife and mother to our boys. Our family was becoming a home as we both were learning how to be a spouse and a parent. Seemingly we were doing everything right.

So WHY? Why did God allow this tragedy to happen to our family? The rest of our family would now be watching to see if this new-found faith in God was real. I thought that God was punishing me for the years of my wild living apart from Him. After all, I deserved it, but not Joann; she didn't run from God; she had done nothing wrong. She, just recently, shared with me her feelings that Johnny's birth defects were somehow her fault. So we played the blame game for a while, but we eventually discovered the reality that it wasn't our fault, but "unique multiple malformations" that had caused all of Johnny's problems.

Then all the other questions began to flood our hearts: Would he have a speech impediment? Would Johnny have any friends? Would the other kids pick on him? Would he have a girlfriend? Would he go to prom? I finally had to stop myself from thinking too far ahead. There were too many things to take care of today, to be worried about the long term. The Bible says in; Matthew 6:34 *"Take therefore no thought for the morrow: for the morrow shall take thought for the things of itself. Sufficient unto the day is the evil thereof."*

To anyone who may be in a similar situation today, the old saying, "one day at a time" is so true. It is very easy to get caught up in all the tomorrows that may never come. Try not to allow yourself to dwell in the future. Today will be hard enough to deal with. And if by chance today is a good day, ENJOY IT! We can ruin a good today by fretting about the rough tomorrows. Believe me, I am the king of destroying a perfectly good day by prioritizing tomorrows. The truth is, tomorrow may never come, and if it does come, it will have its own set of issues to be dealt with. Focus on today and let tomorrow take care of itself. I heard an old pastor once say, "Worry is like a rocking chair. It doesn't get you anywhere, but it gives you something to do." Very true words.

As we struggled to find the answer to the "why?" question, it was our other sons that asked the much more practical questions. After two weeks in I.C.U., Johnny came home to meet his brothers. Bob and Jason were so sweet. They were at the age where they were still so innocent and just wanted to see their new brother. We tried to prepare them by showing them his picture and explaining to them that he had a hole in his face that the doctors would fix.

When they first met Johnny they loved him right away. His oldest brother Bobby asked, "Does it hurt?" Jason wanted to know "Who did this to him?" and "if Johnny was going to die?" Great questions from an eight and five year old.

So many questions enter our minds at times like this. The biggest question is "Why?", but we also want to know the answers to the "What?" questions. What caused this to happen? What will be in the future? Again, most of our questions go unanswered when we ask them. We try to figure out all the possible scenarios and most of the time we are wrong in all our predictions.

There is one question that I would like to address that is asked less frequently, but the answer is more readily available. That is the "Who" question. Who allowed this to happen? Who made my child this way? The answer many times seems counter intuitive, but the real answer is that God created our son the way He did for

In Spite Of

His purposes. I tell you the truth, that was a hard concept to accept for my wife and me. I mean, how could our God that loves us and our son, bring this life into existence with so many problems? How could He bring so much pain into our lives?

I had a conversation with a neighbor not long after Johnny was born. Well, let's say it was more of a confrontation than a conversation. She had seen a preacher on the television that said that birth defects are from the Devil and that our son was born with all his problems because he was made that way by Satan. Well needless to say, I wasn't too happy with the direction of our conversation and advised her that she should probably stop watching that preacher and get into her Bible.

Theologically, it is easier to accept that these things happen as a result of the Devil's attack on us. The idea of God bringing or allowing such pain and suffering is a hard idea to reconcile. However, if we would look into the "perfect law of liberty", we can see that God is the creator of all things for His purposes. Moses was called of God to lead the nation of Israel out of Egypt, but Moses wasn't too keen on the idea, so he told the Lord he wasn't eloquent of speech and that God needed to find someone else. God's response is quite telling; Exodus 4:11 *"And the Lord said unto him, Who hath made man's mouth? or who maketh the dumb, or deaf, or the seeing, or the blind? have not I the Lord?"* Having a son with a cleft lip and palate I found that reading those words hit me hard, as most Bible truths do.

There is an account in the New Testament of a man that was born blind and Jesus' disciples asked Him who had sinned, this man or his parents because he was born blind? In other words, they assumed that this man's defects were somehow related to sin. Jesus puts that way of thinking to rest in John 9:3 *"Jesus answered, Neither hath this man sinned, nor his parents: but that the works of God should be made manifest in him."*

We spend so much time trying to figure out the "Why" and the "What" when we need to look to the "Who". The Lord has a purpose behind all that comes into our lives, even our pain and sorrow. My favorite Bible character is Job. The book devoted to his testimony helped get me through the first few months of Johnny's life. I immersed myself in God's Word trying to make sense of all that was happening to us. I had heard of this person that I thought was a "superhuman" and wondered how he could have endured what he went through, while staying faithful to God.

As I read this powerful account of Job's reaction to unimaginable pain, I realized he was human after all. Not a "superhuman." He was just a man that grieved deeply over his loss and hated even the day he was born, but stayed true to God. In spite of his deep pain and agony, he kept his focus on the Lord. He didn't always react in a perfect way, but he knew his strength came from the Lord.

Job had a group of friends that blamed his sin for his trials and a wife that told him to "curse God and die". However, Job knew that somehow God had a plan in all of it, even though he didn't know what it was. He would believe God was in control.

Job 23:10 "But he knoweth the way that I take: when he hath tried me, I shall come forth as gold."

We won't always get our answers when we want them, and many times the answers we get aren't the ones we are looking for. We may never fully know the "Why" or the "What", but we can always trust in the "Who". Joann loves a quote that she read somewhere: "God gives us something better than the answers to our questions, He gives us Himself." It is He that allows our trials, and it is He that will sustain us through them. Although Job's children all had a special place in his heart and he no doubt loved them all, their stories ended in the first chapter of the book. The story of Job's faith is the primary message of the rest of the book. Job kept his integrity throughout his grief and pain. His life not only affected those living in his day, but some thirty five hundred years later, his legacy is helping people today.

Whatever it may be that we are going through today, we must keep our eyes on the "Who", not on the "Why" or "What", so that we can endure the pain we feel today and, like Job, keep our integrity.

In Spite of our Faith

Chapter Three

The Need to Talk In Spite of an Empty Room

James 1:19 *"Wherefore, my beloved brethren, let every man be*
swift to hear, slow to speak, slow to wrath:"

Listening to others is a lost art today. Most of the time we are listening for an opportunity to speak. When a person experiences a loss they have an incredible need to speak about that loss. Whether it is the loss of a loved one, a job, or a dream, there is a need to talk it out…..often. It is a rare and caring person that will open themselves up to allow others that are hurting to share their pain. They leave themselves vulnerable to feeling another's sorrow, which for most is not something to which we aspire.

As I mentioned earlier, Joann and I didn't freely express our feelings to each other early on in our grief. We both were afraid of expressing an attitude of outrage toward God. We suppressed our feelings of anger and doubt that God cared about what we were going through. It is only natural to wonder why God was working in our lives the way He was, yet we could never seem to express those feelings to anyone.

In Spite Of

A few weeks after Johnny's birth, we finally had a visit from our pastor. He and his wife came over and we were ready to talk. They were very sweet and intelligent people, who had helped us develop into a Christian family. We thank God for their example and leadership in our early years as Christians. Their visit with us wasn't long and we talked about many things from baseball to the church. The pastor even made a comment about how Johnny looked like his dad in a very weak attempt at some humor. Before we knew it, the visit was over. There was no mention of what we were going through; no asking of how we felt. We couldn't believe it! We never had the opportunity, that we needed so badly, to speak about our feelings and how we thought about our God. This seemed so odd, very difficult and disappointing for us.

Feelings of isolation began to overcome us. You see, it wasn't just the pastor that wouldn't give us opportunity to talk about the heartache we were feeling. We soon found that most people didn't want to talk about it or would just avoid us altogether. We literally lost contact with many of our close friends. Those that we did stay in touch with didn't ask the questions that would lead us into a conversation about all we were experiencing. Whether it was because they didn't know what to say, or didn't want to stir up sad feelings in us, we were left with very few friends that would open up and let us talk.

Then there were the people that had the advice. They would listen long enough to formulate an opinion and give us a solution after just a few minutes. The hardest people for me to deal with were the people that always wanted to quote Scripture. Romans 8:28 became a verse that would cut through my heart like a knife. Remember in the recovery room, Joann asked me "How could something that hurts so bad be good?" We knew the Scriptures!!! But knowing the Scriptures didn't make the pain go away. There is great comfort in the Word of God when you are dealing with pain in your life. However, when you are hurting you don't need to be preached to.

In Spite of an Empty Room

Not having someone to talk to about your grief is far from unusual; as a matter of fact it is the norm! In many of the support groups that we have attended, most of the people express the same experiences: no one to talk to, or those that do allow you to talk want to offer advice. For the most part, those giving the advice have no clue what you are going through.

The greatest thing that you can do for someone in grief is to listen. They don't need nor do they want advice from people. Their story just needs to be told. It needs to be told more than once, it needs to be told again and again.

I would like to encourage anyone that has a loved one that is grieving for one reason or another, let them talk to you. Ask them how they are doing and mean it. Don't accept the "I'm fine" or "I'm good" answers. You see, those that are hurting have conditioned themselves to say what people want to hear rather than tell the truth. They don't want to sound like they are complaining or to suck the joy out of a room. They don't want to chase away the few friends they have left by talking about their grief. In an effort to spare other people's feelings, they have learned to suppress their own. This only hurts them and prolongs the grieving process.

There is another group of people that want to always make comparisons to pain. They mean well, but comparing pain is kind of foolish. They will start a sentence with, "That's just like…", but after they have finished telling their story it is really nothing like the pain you are going through. Joann and I always would try to find humor in this comparison game. Our son suffered for years with severe back and knee pain. He had kyphosis and scoliosis of the spine which caused him a great deal of pain. People would compare pain meds and treatments with us and tell us how bad they have it. We would always claim them to be the winners of the pain competition.

In Spite Of

When Johnny went to heaven it was by far the most difficult trial we have ever had to face. We prayed, at his request, for two years that God would take him home to relieve his pain and on October 3, 2015, God answered our prayers. However, if I had known how badly it would hurt to lose him, I don't know that I could have prayed that way. After twenty-eight years of being with Johnny, virtually twenty-four hours a day, seven days a week, he was gone.

We know based on the Word of God that Johnny is with Jesus in heaven. We are eternally grateful for the blessed hope of heaven, but, that doesn't make us miss him any less. Many times friends, in an attempt to comfort us will say, "We know he is not suffering anymore." And this is true, but we are, and the pain is unimaginable.

We recently heard a person that was grieving the loss of two of her daughters talk about "putting on the mask" everyday so those around her wouldn't feel uncomfortable. I had never heard it explained that way before, but Joann and I knew exactly what she meant. People don't want to be around someone who is sad most of the time. So you just put up a good front, and in the private times take the mask off and grieve. As a pastor it is expected of you to get back to being yourself quickly. Your grief and sorrow have an expiration date. I was speaking with a fellow pastor recently whose wife had just gone through treatments for cancer. He shared with me his feelings that he was expected to "Man up" because he was a Baptist Pastor. This dear man has five daughters. He was busy caring for them, his wife and a large church at the same time. Man up? We far too often put the expectations of others before what God expects of us. Remember He knows how we feel.

Hebrews 4:15-16 " For we have not an high priest which cannot be touched with the feeling of our infirmities; but was in all points tempted like as we are, yet without sin.16 Let us therefore come boldly unto the throne of grace, that we may obtain mercy, and find grace to help in time of need."

In Spite of an Empty Room

People will compare the death of another loved one, even the loss of a family pet. No one knows our grief except that of another parent that has lost a child. Even those of us that have lost children have stories that are all different, but, the grief for all of us is at times overwhelming.

You see there is no reason to compare pain and grief. I read somewhere that the "worst kind of grief is the grief you are going through". The worst kind of grief is not losing a child or getting diagnosed with cancer. It is the grief you are experiencing at the time. Your grief is the worst grief you can experience.

Grief must be talked about. That is why support groups are so vital. You can get around people that are going through similar situations; people that truly know your pain. Not everyone grieves the same way and it is impossible to know how another person feels, but at least you have an opportunity to talk about your situation. If you are experiencing a type of grief today, do some research and find a support group that best fits your scenario and attend, talk and listen; it will do you a world of good.

For us, each support group we have attended over the years have had their own set of challenges. Each was a place that we could talk, but many of them didn't fill the bill for us. When Johnny was an infant we attended a cleft palate support group. That group had families dealing with cleft palate issues only. Kidney transplant support groups only talked about kidney issues. Deaf support groups talked about deaf issues. We never truly fit in anywhere because of the extensive medical issues Johnny had. The isolation kept getting deeper for us until we just decided that we would rely on our God.

Today we attend The Compassionate Friends support group for those that have lost a child. It is such a blessing to share Johnny's story with them and have a venue in which we can talk among people that know how important listening is. Every person there has a different story to tell, yet we all share the same loss, and it has been healing as we talk it out.

Please don't misunderstand, we do have dear friends that have through the years listened to us. They will ask the questions and are prepared and willing to hear the truth. We are so grateful for their open hearts. They have encouraged us down through the years more than they know.

One friend, in particular, that has listened to me over and over again, I met at work when he was going through a divorce that almost killed him. He was a crushed soul. After twenty-seven years of marriage his wife filed for divorce. I met with him every day during lunch and listened, again and again. He had no one to talk to but me at the time and we became very close friends, even to this day. We had a great arrangement though, in that, he also let me talk to him about our struggles with Johnny and how we were hurting as Johnny was hurting. We would take turns having bad days. We would joke that we hoped we wouldn't both have a bad day at the same time. Butch and I still lean on each other. Through Johnny's death he was there for me and has allowed me the opportunity to talk.

There is also a couple who has been such a huge blessing to Joann and me. We have been friends with them since we were in high school. Through the years we have had children, moved close to each other, and far away from each other. However, we have always remained as close friends. When Johnny went to heaven, Bob and Linda came to the funeral and asked what they could do to help. I looked them in the eyes and said, "Please, stay close. The funeral will come to an end and we are going to need your friendship now more than ever." Thankfully, they heard me and have gone out of their way to stay close. We go out for dinners once a month and they give us their time. We call it our monthly "Therapy Session". We laugh and we cry, but we can just be real and enjoy their friendship, and hopefully they enjoy ours.

Our dear pastor and his wife have also been a great source of encouragement through the years. Even though I now pastor myself, I sat under Pastor Steve Brown for sixteen years and still look to him for counsel. As I have already stated, we wore them out with hospital visits for Johnny. Pastor Brown knew which candy was Johnny's favorite and would always stop at the gift shop of the hospital and bring him some when he would visit. There was one time, however, that the gift shop was closed and he was unable to bring Johnny his treats. This was not lost on Johnny. He told Pastor Brown he had dementia for forgetting to bring him his candy.

Pastor Brown and his wife, Pam, have been very close friends to Joann and me for the last twenty-five years. They have been with us through many of Johnny's surgeries and have always allowed us to talk about our feelings. They never tried to have any answers, nor did they pretend to know what we were and are going through. At Johnny's memorial service, Pastor Brown in all his honesty, had a theme of "I can't imagine." It was a fitting tribute to Johnny's life and an admission that we all need to realize that we can't imagine what others are experiencing. We are so grateful for their ministry in our lives.

Another couple that has not only allowed us to talk, but has been with us through most of Johnny's life, Chuck and Linda. They would always show up at the hospital for surgeries, recoveries, and when Johnny was in-patient. Many times they would come and just sit with us and "be there" for us. Since Johnny's death they have spent much time with us, sent cards and spent unknown hours in prayer for our family. They have been a great blessing to us.

One thing we have learned as a couple is to talk to each other. In the early days, we didn't want to seem "unspiritual" by talking about our feelings. But we were being untruthful with each other by not sharing how we felt and our thoughts. As time went on, we began to speak about our personal pain and realized that we were both experiencing many of the same thoughts.

I can tell you that Joann and I have had an interdependence upon each other over the years of triumph and tragedy that we have walked through. Together we have been through countless times at the hospital, surgeries, dialysis and watching our son suffer, and finally his home going. By God's grace, we have become a team, a good team, I might add. Our roles have changed from time to time and we have had to learn to adapt to the changes in our lives while caring for Johnny. We learned to not just internalize our thoughts but to speak about them, share them with each other, and we learned to depend upon each other's strength.

The most important person we had to learn to share our feelings with was the Lord. You see He knows our thoughts anyway so trying to pretend that we don't have them is futile. Coming to God and being completely honest isn't the easiest thing to do. We may have to confess our anger toward Him, admit we don't understand and ask Him the "Why" questions. You know what? He can handle it! He is not offended by our anger in times of trial. The "Why" questions don't bewilder Him. Talking things out with the Lord is a step towards healing.

When we read the book of Job and the Psalms, we realize that Job and David had questions, but they were willing to take their questions to God. They didn't always get their answers, but they talked it out with God and were better for it.

When we experience tragedy and grief in our lives, we need to find those that will let us talk. When someone we know is going through a difficult time in life, we need to open ourselves up and allow them to talk, again and again.

In Spite of an Empty Room

Chapter Four

The Medical Education In Spite of a Lack of Knowledge

Psalm 139:14 " I will praise thee; for I am fearfully and wonderfully made: marvellous are thy works; and that my soul knoweth right well."

From the first days of Johnny's life Joann and I had to learn an awful lot of medical terms and procedures that were completely foreign to us, as well to most people really. While he was still in N.I.C.U., we had to learn to gavage feed him. Because of his cleft lip and palate he was not able to suck on a bottle. Gavage feeding involved inserting a tube down his throat into his stomach, ensuring that it was not in his lungs, and then pouring formula into a syringe and allowing gravity to pull the formula through the tube into his stomach in order for him to get nourishment. This was a difficult thing to do throughout the day, but those early morning feedings were especially hard when we were half asleep.

As was mentioned earlier, Johnny came home after two weeks in the hospital and met his brothers for the first time. After only one night at home, we had to take him for his first surgery on his cleft lip. The surgeon was touted as "world renowned" and the

43

In Spite Of

best in our area to work on children with cleft lips and palates. This was to be the first of over forty surgeries that Johnny would endure in his lifetime.

Giving your child over to a surgical team is a very emotional experience. You know that there is always a risk involved with anesthesia and that your child will emerge from the operating room in some way different than they entered. You know they will be in pain and you pray the surgery is a success.

When the surgery was over, Johnny had a bandage across what now was an upper lip. His cheeks were no longer chubby but drawn in and tight. He also had arm restraints on, called "no-no's," hard plastic sleeves that kept his arms straight not allowing him to bend them at the elbow so he wouldn't touch his lip and damage the repair.

We took Johnny home the next day with a follow-up visit to the surgeon's office four days later. On the follow-up visit the surgeon removed the bandage from Johnny's lip to expose a clean upper lip and a small cut line. It was such an improvement over the hole in his face! The doctor removed his stiches and told us to leave the restraints on his arms.

That same night Johnny began crying and when Joann went into his room to see what was wrong, she discovered his lip had begun to break open. She called the surgeon at home and he told her to bring him into the office the next morning. Through the night the lip continued to open and became unattached to his nose on the left side, once again exposing a hole in his face where his lip should be. At the surgeon's office he said there was nothing he could do at that time; it would be like trying to sew together butter. We would need to wait about six months until it healed up before he could try and repair it again. Our hearts were crushed.

In Spite of a Lack of Knowledge

Every trip to the doctor's would bring more bad news. He had bi-lateral inguinal hernias, no tear ducts, and he was "wall eyed," a condition where instead of the eyes being crossed they pointed in two different directions. He also had a horseshoe kidney, meaning the kidneys never separated. We were sent to a cardiologist that told us he had an innocent heart murmur, but the chest x-ray revealed what is known as a diaphragmatic hernia, normally fatal at birth, but Johnny had no outward symptoms. Normally, the intestines invade the chest cavity causing damage to the lungs or heart. The hits just kept coming.

When Johnny was about eighteen months old we were referred to a geneticist to check if they could identify a syndrome that he may fit into. That was one of the very lowest points in our lives. The doctor told us that if he continued on the same growth rate he would be lucky to tie his shoes. He said it would take Johnny ten years to develop into a five-year-old and twenty years to have the abilities of a ten-year-old. He also said, "One good thing is that we know he can hear." He made this statement based upon ringing a bell near Johnny's ear and he turned and looked at it. This doctor turned out to be wrong on most of what he told us. They also could never fit John into any syndrome. They just called it the Johnny Ashley Syndrome, unique multiple malformations, with no real cause. He was made just the way God wanted him to be! Luke 18:27 *"And he said, The things which are impossible with men are possible with God."*

When Johnny was two years old, he only weighed fourteen pounds and was diagnosed as "failure to thrive" (you think?). That's when the doctors decided to insert a gastroscopy tube into his stomach through his belly and we began feeding him through a "button" on his tummy. This really improved his strength and he put on eight pounds in six months.

In Spite Of

Over the next twenty-six years or so there were multiple surgeries and hospitalizations, far too many to try to get into in this book. There are a few very important health issues I would like to discuss though.

I said earlier that Johnny had a horseshoe kidney. Little did we know when they first told us this that he would eventually go into kidney failure and would be in need of a transplant.

As time went on, Johnny's kidney function continued to decrease. We had to go to Children's Hospital in Detroit monthly to have his blood drawn and meet with the nephrologists to discuss his care. We learned many new terms such as: creatinine, BUN, hemodialysis, and peritoneal dialysis. Our knowledge was growing, but so was our anxiety. We also knew that the Bible tells us to "be careful for nothing," but watching and wondering what was going to happen next was, at times, overwhelming.

We have met some of the greatest medical professionals during our years of going to the Children's Hospital. There were many doctors in the kidney department alone that we became close to. They all loved Johnny and his sweet spirit. He was amazing when they would draw his blood. Because of having his blood drawn so often, after time it got harder and harder for those drawing the blood to find a good vein. Johnny would be patient with them (most of the time) and he would point out the veins people have had success with in the past. He would also coach them if they weren't doing it just right. Even though he was deaf he was able to get his point across.

One time I remember he was telling the woman drawing his blood that the tourniquet wasn't tight enough. At first she ignored him, and Johnny would roll his eyes and point to the tourniquet. Finally she got the message and realized he was right.

Johnny was on the waiting list for a transplant for a few

months when his nephrologist wanted to train us to start peritoneal dialysis at home. This would involve hooking Johnny to a machine all night that would clean all the toxins out of his blood that his kidneys should do naturally. We never had to receive the training though.

The call came at about 3 o'clock in the morning. It was Johnny's kidney doctor on the phone. Joann answered half asleep then suddenly sat straight up and hit me and said, "It's a kidney!" As she listened to the doctor she kept saying "Okay, yes, I see…" Then she said "Can you explain all that to my husband?" Joann handed me the phone and the doctor explained that this was a good match and they needed to know if we wanted it. "We will always have your kidney later if we need it." The doctor said. (I was being tested to give Johnny one of my kidneys at the time.) I asked her what she thought. She told me it was a good match and we should go for it. She then asked, "How soon can you get to the hospital?" I told her it might take us a couple of hours. We needed to drop our other boys off at their grandparents, but that was on the way to the hospital. (Thank the Lord for grandparents!)

We raced to the hospital and made it in record time. We rushed in the doors expecting there to be a team waiting to place Johnny on a gurney and rush him into the operating room. (I guess I watch too much television.) We were the only ones in a hurry. There were blood tests to be done, tissue typing, and antibody tests to be done. So we sat in pre-op for what seemed to be hours. In the meantime, our pastor and his wife showed up on a Sunday morning hours before church, to pray with us. (This would also become a routine for our dear Pastor)

So we waited, and as we waited the medical team seemed a little concerned about the heart murmur Johnny had. It had been investigated a few years before and we were told it was an innocent murmur. However, a chest x-ray and heart ultra-sound were done,

In Spite Of

then a new cardiologist came in to speak to us.

We were already on edge worrying about the transplant when he dropped a bomb on us. He told us that Johnny's aortic valve in his heart had a severe leak and that it would eventually need to be replaced. He began giving us too many details about what would need to be done down the road when I stopped him and asked if what he was telling us would prevent the kidney transplant from going forward. He said it would not and gave us his card and informed us that he would be following Johnny through the transplant. Then, when things settled down we would meet at his clinic there in Children's.

I don't remember exactly, but it seemed like the surgery took about three hours. While we were waiting, Joann's mom and dad showed up with our other boys and several friends came to support us and pray. Finally, Johnny's kidney doctor walked out in her scrubs and said, "What's your favorite letter of the alphabet?" After a few seconds and some awkward stares she said, "P! The kidney is working and is making pee!" We all got her sense of humor at the same time and let out a collective sigh of relief. She went on to tell us that the kidney Johnny received was rather large and they had to really stuff it into his small body. We thank the Lord all went well.

Johnny spent several days in Intensive Care recovering from the transplant and getting the right combination of medications to keep him from rejecting the kidney. Once again, he received great care from the medical staff.

The one thing that we had to face that most parents didn't was the fact that Johnny was deaf. We had to be his interpreters, as well as his parents. As he got older and his stays in the hospital became longer, we began to face a lot of the politics and decisions that are made out of a concern for costs in the hospital setting. Providing an interpreter was one of the services that we had to fight for.

In Spite of a Lack of Knowledge

Once Johnny recovered from his transplant we began seeing the cardiologist that had discovered the aortic valve problem. We went every year at first, then every six months, then every other month as the leaky valve became worse. Through the years, we have gotten very close to the different cardiologists that our son has had. Each one had been very compassionate and became very close to us and Johnny. Two of them attended Johnny's memorial service, which was such a blessing to us and showed the impact Johnny had on their lives.

Finally, the day came when the doctor told us that we needed to meet with a heart surgeon to schedule a valve replacement surgery. We knew that day would eventually come, you just never really want to face that serious of a surgery. We met with the pediatric heart surgeon at Children's Hospital, a very kind and soft spoken man that took a lot of time to explain what he would be doing. We asked our questions and he answered them the best he could. There are never any guarantees in any surgery, especially a heart surgery on a kidney transplant patient.

The hospital provided an interpreter for Johnny at that appointment. He watched the interpreter as he signed his best trying to get Johnny to understand. Then the doctor asked if Johnny had any questions, He paused and asked if he was going to use the tool that would spread his rib cage apart during the surgery. I had to interpret that for the interpreter. The doctor was amazed that he would even know about that device and asked, "How does he know about that?" We responded that he watches a lot of the medical shows on television. The surgery was scheduled and we began to pray for God to help the surgeon.

Johnny was always a complicated case, and this surgery would be no different. We had been admitted the day before surgery and were up well before dawn and in pre-op by 6 o'clock in the morning. As usual we appeared much more nervous than Johnny. We all prayed together and they took him into surgery about 6:45. The cardiologist kept an eye on what was going on in surgery and he would periodically come and give us updates as to how the surgery was going. He came out at one point and told us things were going well and they were getting near the end.

After that we waited for quite a while and he came and told us some bad news. They needed to do another surgery on his heart. After the valve was replaced and they took him off the bypass machine, his heart began to relax because it didn't need to work as hard. When that happened part of the heart tissue covered the new valve and was restricting the blood flow. Because of that, they had to put him back on bypass and do another heart surgery.

We later found out through the cardiologist that the surgeon had done some very "heroic" work during the surgery. Altogether, Johnny was in surgery for about 16 hours. By that time we had a large group of family and friends from church gathered together. Finally, the surgeon came and spoke to my Joann and me and explained all that took place then asked who all the people were. We introduced him to Joann's parents and our pastor and explained that many were people from our church. He then asked if we could pray together. He prayed one of the sweetest and most humble prayers I have ever heard. It was obvious to me, he knew where his power and strength came from.

While in intensive care, they were monitoring and pacing Johnny's heart with an external pacemaker. It looked almost like a transistor radio, it had a couple of knobs and some wires that went into John's chest and were connected to his heart. When you're in intensive care there are lots of monitors and IV pumps and a flurry of constant activity. Doctors come and go, interns will many times accompany doctors to learn or to be involved in the case. One such resident doctor would be following Johnny while the surgeon was out of town.

One evening while we were in Johnny's room the resident doctor came in and he decided that Johnny's heart rate was a little low so he adjusted the pacemaker. He then proceeded to connect two of the wires that weren't being used. Suddenly Johnny's heart rate shot up to over 300 beats a minute, his blood pressure bottomed out, and he sat up in bed clenching his chest while all the color left his face! Alarms started going off and the nurses came running. Finally, the doctor unplugged the pacemaker and Johnny collapsed on the bed. At first I thought he was dead, then he signed "I was dreaming." The doctor never said a word and left the room; while Joann and I stood in shock. The nurse that was in charge of Johnny's care was very upset, she didn't say much, but she told us that she included the tape off the EKG monitor in Johnny's records.

When the surgeon returned from his out of town trip, he came into the room and was discussing Johnny's progress with the resident that had had adjusted the pacemaker. The surgeon looked at us and asked us how we thought things were going. I asked if the resident had told him about the incident with the pacemaker. The surgeon hadn't heard anything about it. I was more than happy to tell him about it. The surgeon was visibly upset and had some harsh words for the resident in front of us; I'm sure he had more to say once they left the room. We never saw that resident again. After two weeks Johnny was discharged and we got home and celebrated!

We followed up with the cardiologist a couple of months after surgery and expected a routine visit with good news. However, that isn't how it went. After the normal chest x-ray and echocardiogram we met with the cardiologist, our new friend. He had a pained look on his face and started the conversation with, "I don't know how to tell you this, but Johnny's mitral valve is now leaking." That was another shotgun to the stomach moment. We couldn't believe our ears, "Not another heart surgery!" He went on to explain that the process would be the same as what we went through with the aortic valve until he needed surgery. No real timeline was discussed just watching the valve and seeing how the leak progressed. We were devastated. Joann asked if the incident with the pacemaker after surgery had anything to do with it, and he said it was highly unlikely. Thankfully there was no interpreter there to share this bad news with Johnny that day.

The thought of Johnny going through another heart surgery was hard to accept. Hadn't he been through enough? Watching your child go through pain is a difficult thing. We didn't tell Johnny for quite a while, as going to see the heart doctor for him was a normal part of life. Besides, the girls that did the echocardiograms were cute, and Johnny loved the ladies, so he enjoyed going to Cardio Clinic.

In the years that followed we moved to the western suburbs of Detroit and further from Children's. The move put us almost exactly between Children's in Detroit and Mott's Children's Hospital in Ann Arbor. We loved the people and the care that Johnny was getting in Detroit, but he was getting older and having an interpreter was a high priority with us. We didn't want to be interpreters for every visit to the hospital; we just wanted to be parents. We had been told by other Deaf people we knew that the University of Michigan Hospital provided interpreters for the Deaf at all their clinics. Since Mott's is part of the U of M system they provided interpreters there also.

We began making the transition with most of Johnny's doctors from Detroit to Ann Arbor. The last doctor we were going to transfer would be the cardiologist. We planned on waiting until Johnny's mitral valve was replaced.

The time came once again for us to go and meet with Johnny's heart surgeon. We went through the whole discussion about the risks of the surgery and potential for a lot of bleeding because of the scar tissue from the last surgery. Then the doctor told us that he himself needed back surgery and would not be able to do Johnny's for several months. He wanted to be completely healed to operate on him. Because of all the complications of the prior heart surgery he thought it best to delay it until he was better.

We believed, at that point, that the Lord closed the door for him to do the surgery and that it was time to move Johnny's cardiac care to Mott's in Ann Arbor where all his other specialists were. This was going to be hard for us because we had grown personally fond of Johnny's heart doctor and we thought he might take the move hard. Well, we were right, the doctor was not pleased. He was actually mad about it. He didn't understand our reasons at first and tried to talk us out of it. But, our minds were made up. We truly believed God wanted Johnny's care and the upcoming surgery at the U of M. Reluctantly he gave his blessing.

A few days later the cardiologist from Detroit called and said he had a good friend at Mott's that he would recommend. He also informed us that he would mail us Johnny's echocardiograms to take with us to the new doctor. This was our last doctor from Detroit that we had to transfer and it was hard for us also. He was a great doctor.

The cardiologist at Mott's proved to be another great doctor and quickly became a friend. He followed Johnny even after he was transferred to the adult hospital. Every time Johnny was in-patient, Dr. Ensing would come from Mott's to check on Johnny just to see how he was doing. He wasn't even in charge of Johnny's care and would go out of his way to see Johnny and us.

The time finally came for Johnny to have the mitral valve replaced. He was going to be in the care of a world renowned pediatric heart surgeon. We had our consultation with him and the kidney transplant team were all on board. Then the date for surgery was set.

In Spite Of

We were admitted a couple of days before surgery so they could get Johnny off his blood thinners and be sure his kidney was hydrated. The morning of the surgery we met briefly with the heart surgeon. He told us that Johnny was going to be his second surgery that day. Our friends and family began to gather at the hospital. Our pastor and his wife once again were there with us waiting for the okay to take Johnny to pre-op. We waited and waited; then finally a nurse came in and said, "We have to cancel the surgery. The first surgery didn't go well and the surgeon doesn't want to operate in his state of mind." We understood, but what an emotional rollercoaster.

Later a doctor came in and explained to us our options. We could go home and reschedule with the original surgeon or have his associate do the surgery in the morning. After a brief word of prayer and discussing it with each other, we felt that since we were already at the hospital and Johnny was prepared medically, we would have it done the next day.

In the morning the new surgeon met with us and explained the procedure that he wanted to try on Johnny. He was very passionate in his explanation. He said that he could go in through Johnny's rib cage and collapsed his lung and the valve should be right there for him to replace. This was a completely different procedure than the other two surgeons had planned. They were going to go through the front of his chest and open his sternum again. This would have been very bloody and the recovery would have taken another two weeks in the hospital.

The surgery went as the doctor had planned and he was very satisfied. We were surprised at how quickly Johnny recovered this time in comparison to the last heart surgery. Johnny was back home within a week and a half and not in as much pain as before. Through all the changes, different hospitals, changing surgeons, and making some hard decisions based on what we felt to be God's leading. God showed us that He was always in control. We are so grateful that we yielded to His leading. Proverbs 16:9 " A man's heart deviseth his way: but the Lord directeth his steps."

Over the next few years there were some minor surgeries and several hospitalizations with bouts of pneumonia. Through it all, the grace of God was evident in our lives as He strengthened us and Johnny; and encouraged us to take each day as it came, and not to look too far ahead. Suddenly, after seventeen years, Johnny's kidney transplant began to fail. This was actually very remarkable because most kidney transplants from a deceased donor only last five to ten years. Johnny became very sick and it took a lot of the fight out of him.

Our son Jason and I began the process of being tested to see if we could donate one of our kidneys to Johnny. I would be the most likely candidate, then Jason would be the second option if I was not cleared to give one of my kidneys. The testing found that I had kidney stones, so I was not an option. We all as a family had to have serious discussions about the wisdom in giving Johnny a kidney.

Johnny's health took that decision out of our hands. His heart was having some serious issues and he was not very healthy. As a matter of fact, they decided not to put Johnny on the transplant list because he was so ill. Johnny had even told the family he didn't want Jason to give him a kidney because of his poor health. He was always so aware and in tune with his own body. He also always had such a big heart for his brothers.

He then began his journey on dialysis three times a week. This would be his lot in life every Monday, Wednesday, and Friday-four hours in a chair, hooked up to a dialysis machine. This was when Johnny began to give up on his dreams. He always talked of being married and living independently; however, he realized that dialysis was a game changer for him. His dreams were dashed and life was as good as it was going to be for him.

In Spite Of

Over the two years that Johnny was on dialysis, he went through four tunneled catheters (that is what was used for his dialysis access), he had three infections, and spent weeks in the hospital. It was felt that his heart couldn't handle the additional blood flow when he first began dialysis, so the tunneled catheter was the best option for him.

Over time his heart began to improve and the decision was made to put in a fistula for his dialysis treatments to cut down on infections. The fistula was created and Johnny had healed from the surgery. However, the fistula would never be used. The day before Johnny went to heaven, we got the phone call that Johnny had been cleared and listed for another transplant. But, God had different plans for him. Revelation 21:4 *"And God shall wipe away all tears from their eyes; and there shall be no more death, neither sorrow, nor crying, neither shall there be any more pain: for the former things are passed away."*

Through the process of time a caregiver becomes an expert in the medical issues that the one they care for is dealing with. Managing medications, doctor appointments and their care at home is a full time job. It is a wise medical professional that will listen to a caregiver regarding their patients. There are those that won't listen to a laymen caregiver, but the wise ones will. This usually works well for everyone; especially the patient. After all, the well being of the patient is the goal of both the doctor and the caregiver.

In Spite of a Lack of Knowledge

In Spite Of

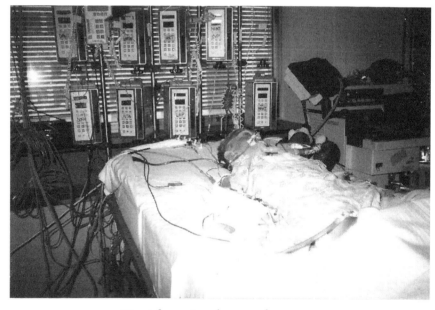

First heart valve replacement
at Detroit Childrens Hospital (2000)

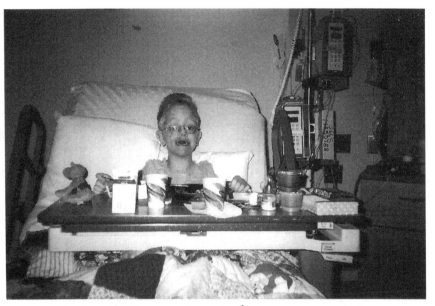

Sitting up to eat after surgery

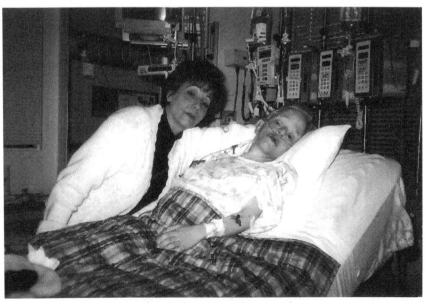

Recovery from heart valve replacement

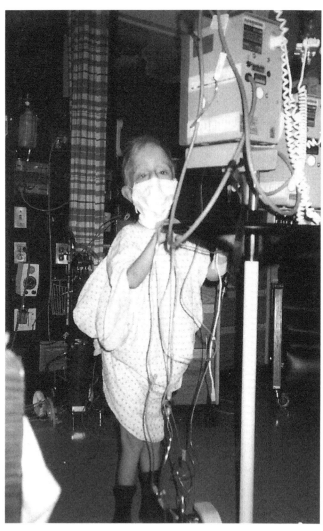

Beginning to walk the halls after
kidney transplant surgery

Discharge day! Home Sweet Home

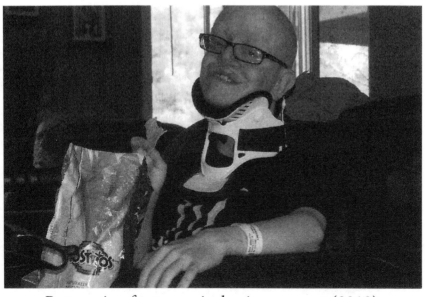

Recovering from cervical spine surgery (2012)

Chapter Five

Strength In Spite of Weakness

Romans 8:18 " For I reckon that the sufferings of this present time are not worthy to be compared with the glory which shall be revealed in us."

As I have already mentioned, it is very difficult to watch your child suffer. If it were possible Joann and I would have gladly taken Johnny's pain upon ourselves. However, the reality is, we never really knew how much physical pain he was in. Johnny experienced pain his entire life. We don't know if he ever had a pain free day. He was truly the strongest person we have ever met. Even though his little body was weak and frail, God had given him an inner strength that we have never witnessed in any other human. 2 Corinthians 4:16 " *For which cause we faint not; but though our outward man perish, yet the inward man is renewed day by day."*

From his first days on earth until his last, Johnny hurt. From the many surgeries, or from the malformation of his body, pain was his daily companion. The physical pain was most times evident even though for the most part he didn't complain. I believe worse than the physical though was the emotional pain that Johnny went through almost daily.

Johnny was not blind to the fact that he was very different from everyone else. He could see the stares he would get from other people, especially children in their natural curiosity, would stare holes through Johnny. Many times I would position myself between him and those that would stare. There were times we were thankful that he was deaf so he wouldn't hear the things children would say, but he knew they were looking and he could read their faces well.

All his life he just wanted to be "normal." He wanted to be able to do the things his brothers did. Even in school he would try to participate in gym. I will never forget arriving at his school to pick him up for a doctor's appointment and seeing him on the track waddling trying his best to finish a lap. He wore braces on both his legs and I knew that they were probably rubbing his legs raw and he was most likely in a lot of pain. It brought me to tears, but it was just an example of the spirit he had. That is what the other kids were doing so that is what he was going to do.

We know that the Lord gave us the strength required for taking care of Johnny for so many years. I read many years ago that marriages that have a disabled child born into the family will end in divorce at an alarming rate. I believe the statistics showed that about 80% of these marriages break up. It is not surprising to me that many marriages can't handle the stress related to caregiving for a special needs child. It can be overwhelming for a parent, especially if one parent is the primary caregiver. This is not unusual because many times the mother is the one who has to go to all the doctor appointments and is in charge of taking care of the needs of the child. Most of the time the financial pressure falls on the father and he feels the responsibility of being the sole provider for the family. The bills mount up and things can get tight really fast.

In Spite of Weakness

I always say that "life" happens to everyone, meaning that we all have our share of challenges that come into our lives from time to time. The car breaks down, the kids need braces, the bills mount up. You get the picture. Now add the stress of needing to care for a special-needs child or even an aging parent. The stress in the family goes to a new level. The problem is that most of the time we don't recognize it while we are living it. That is when the family can begin to come apart if we don't find the strength needed to deal with "life" and the extra stress we have been given.

I was operating a small commercial heating business out of our home when Johnny was born. This allowed me to help my wife with many of the challenges that lay ahead for us, but it also was an added stressor, in that the business wasn't doing well. As a matter of fact, that business eventually failed as well as another attempt at a different business. I ended up working two jobs and we almost lost our home in the process. "Life" happened while we were attending to Johnny's needs. We also had two other boys that needed a mom and dad to love them.

I can honestly tell you that looking back, I don't see how we could have survived all that went on for so many years without the Lord. He has been the source of our strength for all this time. That's not to say everything has been perfect. Like most couples, we have had the normal marital struggles and our family went through the turbulent teen years with our other two sons. However, our family has remained strong and we all have great relationships with one another. For this I give God all the glory!

There was a period of time between Johnny's transplant and his first heart surgery that was particularly difficult. For any number of reasons, Johnny started to become violent. He didn't want to get on the bus for school, he refused to go to church and he just wouldn't obey. He would kick and pull your hair and bite. At that time he was only about 10 years old and very small for his age, yet he was incredibly strong. I had to change my shifts at my job to protect Joann from having to fight with him in the mornings before school.

It all started when he was in the hospital for a surgery. I arrived at the hospital after my shift at work and as I entered the floor I could hear my wife yelling at the nurses to get some help for her in his room. This was so far out of character for her it surprised me to hear her speaking like that. We met at the nurse's station and she was in tears telling me that Johnny had hit her in the eye and he was out of control. I left her at the nurse's station and went to Johnny's room to find four nurses holding him down to his bed and yelling at him. I told the nurses to let him go. I said, "He speaks with his hands and he can't say anything while you are holding his arms!" They looked at me like I was crazy, then they released him. Johnny was shaking with rage and grabbed his IV line and bit it in half. After that he seemed to calm down as saline was pouring all over his bed from the broken line. I calmly reached over and clamped off the line and signed "Are you happy now?" He just started sobbing and I held him in my arms and we had a good cry together.

We don't know whether it was the culmination of all the surgeries or his deafness or the steroids they were giving him, but most likely it was a combination of everything that seemed to push him over the edge. He spent the next six months or so having angry outbursts almost daily. You can only imagine the wear and tear that puts on a family.

It was about that time in our home that our oldest son, Bob, and I were having a heated conversation over something that probably was not all that earth shattering, and I said to Bob, "Your Mother and I don't need this from you right now. Can't you see what we are going through?" I will never forget his response as long as I live. He said, "Yeah, well we're going through it too Dad!" Those words went straight to my heart. I realized that I had totally missed the fact that our other sons were suffering right along with us. It was their brother that was having all the problems, and their parents that were dealing with the violence, but their lives were also turned upside down with all the pain we had been going through as a family. I could only bow my head, cry and ask his forgiveness. I had neglected to see the pain that, Bob, and his brother, Jason, were experiencing themselves.

God has blessed us with great sons and Johnny with two great brothers. Bob and Jason didn't give us much trouble at all. They cared for their baby brother all the time. They would take him with them to places they were going and they were never ashamed of their brother Johnny. By God's grace and by His power we all got through those months of violence. We may have been a little battered and bruised by them, but we got through them.

You may be asking, "What happened to change the violence?" Well, through circumstances directed by the Lord, we began a Deaf ministry at our church and I began teaching Johnny and another deaf couple the Bible through sign language. I wasn't very good at signing so I had to teach at a slow pace which turned out to be good for all of us. Through the process of time the Word of God began to open up for Johnny and one day he understood that he was a sinner. Before he would say he was an angel and put a halo over his head with his hands. He realized that these violent episodes were wrong and he needed God's forgiveness. In that Sunday School class he asked God to forgive him and received Jesus Christ as his Savior. The next morning he got on the bus without a fight. Not to say he was never angry again, but the violence stopped and never returned.

I have always told Joann through the years that each new challenge that comes our way is a new opportunity to experience the grace of God. She at times doesn't want to hear that because the pain is real and the fact of the matter is that we have had to draw on His grace more often than we would have liked to. But God's grace and strength has held us up and together through some very difficult times. When He allows our faith to be tested, he gives us the grace we need to endure.

The Apostle Paul was faced with many challenges in his ministry. One particular problem that he had was what he termed the "thorn in his flesh." He had asked the Lord to take it from him three separate times. God's answer is recorded in   2 Corinthians 12:9 *" And he said unto me, My grace is sufficient for thee: for my strength is made perfect in weakness."* It truly is sufficient at all times.

Today as we navigate through the grief of Johnny graduating into heaven, the presence and grace of God is more evident than ever before. We have had an inner peace that has accompanied our grief. (Buckets of tears have been followed by a sense of God's presence with us, which many times has brought more tears.) Not so much tears of sorrow, but tears of knowing that our heavenly Father is with us and there to bring us comfort in times of trial. There is comfort in knowing that there is a purpose to the pain and God is working in our difficult circumstances.

2 Corinthians 1:3 " Blessed be God, even the Father of our Lord Jesus Christ, the Father of mercies, and the God of all comfort;"

In Spite of Weakness

Chapter Six

Laughter In Spite of the Tears

Proverbs 17:22 " A merry heart doeth good like a medicine: but a broken spirit drieth the bones."

Through the twenty-eight years of caring for Johnny we had our share of pain and sorrow. However, we had a lot more laughs and joy than heartache. Our home, for the most part, was a fun place to live. As many of you that have been caregivers know, there can be a twisted sort of humor in our situation. Our family had a way of finding a laugh in the midst of many of our trials.

Johnny himself was one who would love to make people laugh. He would find novel ways to bring humor into his and our lives. Even when you would think he would feel sorry for himself, the sense of humor God put into him would come shining through.

One of the surgeries that Johnny had to have on his cleft lip was called an Abbe Flap. This involved taking a pie shaped piece of his lower lip and grafting it on to his upper lip. In order for the graft to have enough blood flow for it to heal and grow, the upper and lower lips were left connected in the middle for a few weeks.

In Spite Of

It kept his mouth closed in the middle and open on the two sides. This made eating what small amounts of food he ate very difficult and anything that he wanted to drink he had to sip through a straw. He found that he could entertain us all by sticking his tongue out on both sides of his mouth alternating back and forth mimicking a magic trick. When he saw that it made us laugh he would do it in front of all our friends and family.

As Johnny got older he had to have an upper dental plate made so that he could have a better bite. Because of the cleft, his front teeth hadn't come in properly, so he had need of the upper plate. He would always keep moving it around in his mouth clicking it, not knowing that we hearing people could hear the noise it was making. At times we would let him know that the noise he was making was distracting us and he would say he was sorry and go back to whatever he was doing. Other times he would look at us and with his tongue move the plate up and down quickly while rotating his hand around his ear as though he was turning a crank, imitating the wind up false teeth toy that would chatter and bounce across the table. He actually got quite good at that after a while.

Before Johnny's kidney transplant he was fed with a "G" tube, we had a pump that would put a formula into his stomach through a tube in his belly. This caused him to be very constipated; as a matter of fact he was in diapers until he was nine years old. We were continually giving him enemas and using suppositories (which Johnny called bullets) and stool softeners to get him to have bowel movements. Well, when Johnny would have a bowel movement we called it a "code brown" in our home and we would have a little celebration for him.

After Johnny had his kidney transplant, he began to eat for the first time in his life. One of his first meals that he ate while he was still in the hospital was a salad. He fell in love with salads with French dressing on them. With each bite he would hum with enjoyment as he chewed on the lettuce and began tasting food for what we believe was the first time in his life. Joann and I would just sit there watching him eat in pure amazement. As if seeing him eat wasn't enough, eating food also started clearing up his bowel problem. One night after we had gotten home from the hospital we had a major "code brown!" We could see that he was trying to "evacuate" himself so we laid him on a blanket and put a diaper under him in an attempt to make him comfortable. Well, when he finally was able to go he let out a shout of relief and we were amazed at the size of his creation. That was the beginning of him getting out of the diapers and getting "regular."

As I mentioned earlier, Johnny's brothers were perfect for him. The Lord made them all very close and Bobby and Jason treated Johnny like any other younger brother. They helped make him all boy. They knew that Johnny had limitations, and they always seemed to be able to push his limits, as well as his buttons.

Jason, being the middle child, always seemed to have his ways of aggravating his little brother while claiming innocence. When we would travel in the car, Jason had a way of getting Johnny mad and he would yell at Jason. Remember, Johnny was deaf, so he couldn't just say what was happening. But, he had a certain yell he would let out and we knew Jay was up to something. So mom or I would say, "Jason, leave Johnny alone!" His response was always the same, "I'm not doing anything!" Our yearly trips to Florida to visit my mom could be quite long with those two sitting together.

Bobby was the oldest brother, so, once he got his license, he had the responsibility to drive his brothers around when their mom and I were busy. There were times that Bobby would take Johnny out with him to just "hang out," mostly at the mall. One such trip to the mall as they sat watching the people go by, Bob began teaching his brother to rate the girls on a graduating scale from one to ten; this eventually became Johnny's way of rating everything in his life from food to how he felt. That scale became rather handy throughout the rest of Johnny's life.

There was another time that both Johnny's brothers took him to the mall. (It was one of his favorite places to go.) Jason was pushing him in his wheelchair and as they approached a woman's lingerie store Johnny covered his eyes keeping himself from seeing the images in the store window. Jason (always the instigator) turned his chair and gave it a push into the store! Johnny uncovered his eyes to discover he was inside the store and as fast as he could he backed his wheelchair out of the entrance.

As I previously stated; Johnny loved the ladies! One of the things he did enjoy about his hospital visits was that young nurses would take care of him and each one would become the new loves of his life. Well then there were the interpreters that would come and there were also the pretty doctors. As you can see, he was a very fickle young man. One time when Johnny was very sick while in the U of M hospital, he had contracted one of his dialysis line infections. In the middle of the night his blood pressure bottomed out and his oxygen saturation went very low and he had a difficult time breathing. I called for the nurse and she called the "Rapid Response Team." As they worked on him feverishly, a young nurse was holding his hand trying to comfort him. He was in distress and I was thinking, "He would love this attention from this cute nurse if he only wasn't so sick." After they stabilized him, they took him off to intensive care where he spent the next few days.

After he started feeling better he asked me, "Where is the nurse that was holding my hand?" I couldn't believe it! He not only remembered that there was a pretty nurse holding his hand, but could describe her to a tee. We asked around about who she might be and thought she was part of the "Rapid Response Team." We couldn't find her and Johnny got better, but he never forgot that nurse. About a year later Johnny was an in-patient once again and that same nurse came into his room. The nurse remembered Johnny and the night of his emergency, and Johnny certainly remembered her. They both shared a love for horror movies which sent Johnny into orbit over her. She only cared for him for the one night but it was probably his favorite night in the hospital.

Hospitalizations and surgeries can be very exhausting for the family. Sometimes you can get a little punchy from not getting much sleep. After Johnny's first heart surgery, while he was still in intensive care, Joann and I were in the waiting room while the nurses changed shifts and gave report on their patients. I had just finished some mints that were in a hard plastic container. I took the empty box and hid it in my hand while pretending to crack my neck. As I twisted my head with my hands I crushed the plastic box which made a loud cracking sound. While I was doing that a young boy came around the corner and his eyes got as big as saucers and he said, "Dang!" He thought that I was really cracking my neck. I showed him the plastic box so he wouldn't think I broke my neck. This just struck a funny bone in Joann and me and we laughed uncontrollably for several minutes. Tears flowed down our faces and sore stomachs followed. That really helped us relieve some of the stress of being in the hospital.

When Johnny was about twenty years old, Joann's parents began to need more attention. They were forgetting things and not eating properly. They were showing signs of dementia. This was so hard for Joann, not only because of the care that Johnny required, but also because we lived an hour away from them. When we were visiting them one time, the phone rang and I answered it for them. The call was for my mother-in-law. I said, "It's for you Mom," and as I went to hand her the phone, she picked up the remote for the television put it to her ear, and said, "Hello." Johnny realized that grandma had dementia and didn't laugh at the time. However, whenever we would forget something or act in an uncertain way, he was quick to let us know we had dementia. He would let doctors, nurses, interpreters or anyone for that matter know if they had forgotten some information about him that they too were suffering from dementia.

God gave mankind laughter not only for our enjoyment, but as a stress reliever. Many times our family was able to cope with the stress of caring for Johnny with a good laugh. There were several times Johnny would provide the laugh from a hospital bed. One Halloween, while Johnny was in the hospital, he had me bring a Freddy Kruger mask that he had made. He would just sit there in the bed with the mask on waiting for a nurse to come in and react to him. This provided hours of entertainment for him and us.

Before I became a pastor I would get opportunities to preach in different churches that were without a pastor or the pastor was out of town. One such time I was invited to a small church to fill the pulpit. The building was a remodeled one room school house. There was a pretty good sized crowd that morning, so the room was crowded. Joann and Johnny sat in the front row and my wife was interpreting to Johnny as I preached.

Johnny was a notorious clock watcher. He would always keep everyone on time, from teachers to his brothers and us. Without realizing the importance to Johnny, I had not thought of the fact that this church's service started at 11:00am. This may seem no big deal to any of us, but to Johnny it threw his entire Sunday-morning schedule off. You see the church we normally attended started at 10:30 a.m. and we were usually finished well before noon.

As I neared the end of my message I could see out of the corner of my eye Johnny glace at his watch; it was after noon. At that point he quit watching his mother and turned his eyes on me. I knew this was not going to go well, at least for the preacher. I tried to ignore him at first, but this would prove to be impossible. As only Johnny could do, and get away with it, he lifted his left wrist into the air and began pointing at his watch with his right hand while shouting to get my attention. I made an effort to continue preaching but at that point everyone in the room was now looking at Johnny and enjoying watching me try to finish my message. Finally I had to acknowledge Johnny and tell him I knew what time it was and that I was almost done.

As you can imagine the congregation all got a good laugh and probably no one remembers the message but will never forget Johnny. The nice thing was that I was invited back to preach again. There was just one requirement, that I bring my son with me.

Johnny was truly one of the most precious people you could have ever met. Everyone that he spent time with was impressed by his sweet spirit and kind heart. We would tell him that people thought he was precious and he really liked the idea. Especially when the ladies would give him attention. Whether it be at a clinic visit or the grocery store, when people would smile at him, he would ask, "Why are they being so friendly?" We would tell him, "Because they think you are precious."

This led Johnny to begin asking if people thought he was precious. When I would be pushing him through the crowded halls of the hospital and people would make eye contact with him and smile, he would look up and ask, "Do they think I'm precious?" "Yes Johnny, they think you are precious. Everybody thinks you're precious." And precious he was.

It is vital for a caregiver to look for a silver lining in the clouds of constant stress, even when we feel the stress isn't there. That's because the stress is always there. A smile, a laugh, a kind word can go so far in relieving your feelings of being stuck. When I say stuck, I don't mean it in a resentful way; it's like you're just unable to move forward. It's the inability to sometimes make decisions necessary for your personal life because of the needs your loved one

In Spite Of

has. Laugh, cry, let the emotion flow; it will be a type of emotional cleansing for you. It will help you in the day to day struggle with all the responsibility on your shoulders. Remember that a joyful heart is like a medicine.

In Spite of the Tears

In Spite Of

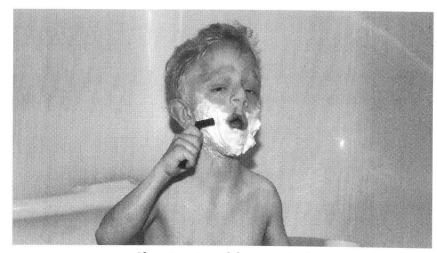

Shaving just like my dad

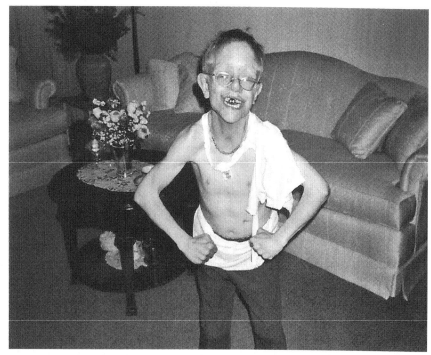

Flexing his guns!

Enjoying Grandma's pool in Florida

Pirouette cookie cigar!

Chapter Seven

Communication In Spite of Silence

Exodus 4:11 "And the Lord said unto him, Who hath made man's mouth? or who maketh the dumb, or deaf, or the seeing, or the blind? have not I the Lord?"

In chapter four I mentioned that we took Johnny to a geneticist and he told us that he could hear because he rang a bell and Johnny turned to look at it. Well, as it turned out, Johnny must have seen the bell out of the corner of his eye because at the age of two and a half he was diagnosed as profoundly deaf. This didn't come as a great shock to us because Johnny was never startled at loud noises. You could call to him and he would never look your way, but if you stomped on the floor he would turn and look in your direction having felt the vibration.

With all the medical problems we were dealing with, deafness was never something that we or the doctors even considered. When we finally had him tested it was a relief to find out he couldn't hear. We now understood the reason why he would not respond to us when we talked to him. However, this would now force our family to learn a whole new way of communication.

In Spite Of

Those of you that have a part in caring for a special needs child understand the politics that can be involved in the education of that child. Labels that we don't like are necessary for proper placement in the special education system. We ran into this due to the fact that Johnny had so many diagnoses. The P.O.H.I. (Physically and Otherwise Health Impaired) program was in a nearby school. However, communication was the most important need for him. It was a fight to get the appropriate special education label so that he could learn to communicate in his language. The special education label for deaf and hard of hearing students is "Hearing Impaired."

We then learned that there are different types of programs for the hearing impaired: Total communication (combination of sign language and voice), S.E.E. (Signing Exact English), Lip reading only, and A.S.L. (Sign language only, the natural, visual, spatial language of the Deaf community, and using A.S.L. grammatical structure versus English word order). That's when we began learning about Individual Educational Program meetings (I.E.P.). For special needs children the process starts early. Again Johnny was two and a half when we found out he was deaf, but his education was already underway.

We are so thankful for the teachers and paraprofessionals that worked with Johnny throughout his years in school. They all have difficult jobs and the way the system works today they spend much of the time they would rather use to work with their students doing paperwork to comply with some government regulations or protecting themselves and the school from lawsuits. God bless all those that work in Special Education.

In order to have Johnny placed in the best program for him, we needed to get his label changed to have hearing impaired as his primary disability. This sounds like it would be an easy thing to do, but it turned into a small battle. I hate to sound calloused but the truth is the money follows the child and when you change labels the money may flow somewhere else. The program Johnny was in was meeting his physical needs but they were trying to educate him through the use of an interpreter which wasn't the best thing for him. Remember he has had no language up until this point and an interpreter was signing what the teacher was saying. However, Johnny got nothing. That is when we learned the magic phrase "Least Restrictive Environment," commonly referred to as LRE. This phrase began to open doors for us and Johnny. It took some time and a couple of I.E.P. meetings, but we finally got Johnny into the hearing impaired program for our area and he began to take off in his education and communication at home.

This also began an education for Joann and myself. As I said earlier, we had to learn a whole new way of communication, so we began taking a sign language class in the evening at Johnny's school. This was a big challenge, especially for me. I didn't do very well in high school Spanish class or my English classes to be truthful and now I had to learn a whole new language? Nothing feels more awkward than trying to use your hands to sign at the beginning. You have to manipulate your fingers in ways you have never moved them before. The entire class felt like we would never be able to learn this manual language and we were all overwhelmed at first.

Eventually we caught on and began to learn to communicate with Johnny. We continued to learn at a pace that kept us on par with his skills. Then Joann decided to get a more advanced education in sign language and attended a local university's sign language classes. As for me, I just stuck with what I could learn from Joann and Johnny.

One of the sad revelations for us was that not many parents of deaf children, especially fathers, took an interest in learning sign language. I wondered, "How would you communicate with your child if you don't understand and speak their language?" I mean, it's not like you can teach them to hear and talk. But, the sad truth is that many deaf children grow up in homes where their language is

In Spite Of

not spoken at all.

Most of the Deaf are by nature very blunt-at times brutally blunt! What is on their mind, they speak. While Joann was taking her sign language class, she became friends with another student that didn't live too far away from our home. This student had been given an assignment to spend time with someone who was Deaf. She asked my wife if she could come to our home and practice by conversing with Johnny. My wife agreed and the appointment was set.

Johnny was not so sure about sitting and talking to some stranger, but he relented and was cordial (for the most part). However, after about an hour of being as polite as he could, Johnny realized that it was almost time for one of his favorite television programs, Rescue 911 (remember he is the clock watcher). He got up from the couch and went and got this woman's coat. He took it, politely placed it in her lap and walked over to the entrance to our home. In a Vanna White type of motion, with both hands, he pointed her to the front door. After we all stopped laughing, she got the not so subtle hint that the meeting had ended. Johnny got to watch his television program and he never saw her again.

Sign language, like any other language, must be used often to be retained in our memory. There are signs that are very inappropriate when used out of context and gestures that could be seen as vulgar. You need to be very careful when signing different words because they can easily be misinterpreted. When Johnny was young he didn't have a good grasp on the "context" of his signs. There was a time when he was in the hospital and his mother and I went to eat in the cafeteria. One of the ladies that worked in chaplain services knew some sign language and heard that there was a deaf patient in the hospital and went to pay Johnny a visit.

At that time Johnny would always sign "morning" when he would meet someone. It seemed to him to be the polite thing to do. The sign involved placing your left hand in the bend of the right elbow and raising your right hand up, representing the sun coming up. When this woman, out of the kindness of her heart, entered into Johnny's room, he signed "morning!" however, it was evening and the sign looked to her as if he had cursed at her so she left in a huff and told the nurses that Johnny had cursed at her.

When Joann and I returned to the room, Johnny was content and sitting in his bed. Then the nurse came in and proceeded to tell us what the lady from chaplain services had said about Johnny cursing at her. We were taken back by the accusation because we were certain that he didn't even know any curse words at that point in his life. (He later developed a small vocabulary of his own.) We then realized that she had mistaken his greeting for some foul language. She knew just enough sign language to be dangerous. We couldn't convince the nurse that he hadn't cursed at her. After all, in her mind the woman from chaplain services "knew sign language."

When Johnny was about ten years old, Joann and I began to pray that the Lord would bring someone to our church that knew sign language so that they could teach our son the Word of God. At that time we were the youth leaders in our church working with the junior and senior high kids and we loved that ministry. As we prayed and earnestly asked God to provide someone to work with our deaf son, the Lord spoke loud and clear to me, "Hey dummy! You and Joann are the only ones in your church that know sign language. You do it!" He may not have used those exact words, but the message was received.

Joann began teaching others in the church sign language and I resigned as youth director to become the Sunday School teacher to our newly formed "Deaf Class". At first the ministry began very slowly with just Johnny and a few hearing folks that would come to class. Then we had a hard-of-hearing couple begin to come and over the next eight years that class grew into a Deaf Church of about fifty people. The Deaf were very patient with me as I struggled through my lessons and sermons in sign and in voice.

We had a good arrangement; they taught me sign language and I taught them the Word of God. One of the things that many deaf people struggle with is the fact that they feel flawed. They don't see themselves as disabled, yet, they are different. Many had gone to churches that would try to heal them of their deafness as though they were made wrong. Some believed the same theology as my neighbor that Satan somehow had created them deaf or that their parents had done something to cause this "affliction" in their lives.

It took some time and a lot of the Bible to show them that they were not flawed or being punished somehow by God. They were created deaf by God, for His glory. The verse I quoted at the beginning of this chapter encouraged many of the deaf members of our church. So many people want to blame God for making them different, yet we celebrate each individual as being unique. Life is not fair, however, if we learn to be content in our state, life can still be rich!

The greatest moment in our deaf ministry for me was when Johnny finally understood the gospel and trusted Christ as his Savior. As I explained in chapter five it changed Johnny's life. Not only did his violence stop, but his eternal destiny was sealed that day and a home in heaven was reserved for him.

Ministering to the deaf was a difficult work for Joann and I. We loved the sweet people that God allowed us to meet and have great memories of our service with them. The difficulty was in the fact that we were daily dealing with our son's medical needs as well as the needs of the deaf church. This became overwhelming as the church grew and Johnny became older. We eventually felt God moving us to another ministry and resigned from the deaf ministry. It was hard saying goodbye but we have many good friends because of our time with the Deaf members of our church.

As a parent of a child who was deaf, I would like to encourage those of you that have given your lives to work with the deaf and hard of hearing. The interpreters that we have known down through the years have been a tremendous blessing to us. We always encouraged Johnny to thank them for their work. They eventually became like family to us. The work that they do is not easy. Many of Johnny's interpreters have been with us in very difficult appointments with doctors. They have had to be the bearers of bad news and have had to fight back their own tears as they told Johnny information that upset all of us. There were times when I know that we violated the "ethics" of interpreting, but we all became so close through the years that sharing our lives with each other became common.

If by chance you are reading this book because you have a deaf child, I really want to impress upon you the importance of learning sign language. Make it the first language in your home. It will not be easy and I can tell you we didn't sign enough in our home. You must realize that much of what we learn in life comes from hearing others talk about a given subject. We may not be directly involved in the conversation ourselves, but we hear others talking and we learn. Johnny would get frustrated with us when we didn't include him in our conversations at home. Many times we would assume that he knew details of an event because we talked about it, yet we didn't sign to include him.

Now imagine yourself in a room full of people and you cannot understand anything anyone is saying. You would feel isolated and think that no one cares about you. Deaf people have told us story after story of being at family gatherings and having no one to talk to. Many of the Deaf people grow up in homes where no one knows sign language but they themselves. Children growing up in homes where they cannot communicate with any of their parents or siblings. Many of the students that attended Deaf schools wouldn't want to leave on Fridays to go home, due to the fact that there was no one to talk to once they would arrive.

For the most part, Deaf people can do anything a hearing person can do. They just communicate in a way that is foreign to the hearing world. They have their own grammatical structure, their own language, and their own culture. The technology of our day has opened up new avenues of communication for them. The Deaf community were some of the first to make the best use of pagers that you could type a message on, email, texting, and social media. Even many elderly Deaf got into new technology long before their hearing contemporaries.

Because of God giving our family a son who was deaf, we all learned a second language, discovered a new culture, and met many new friends that we would have never known otherwise. God also allowed us to minister to many wonderful people and by God's grace we will see many in heaven as a result of the blessing of being part of the deaf world. Johnny's influence on all of us as a family, and those that he inspired throughout his life; has caused us to think of him as a "Silent Hero." His life spoke louder than any words that could have been spoken.

In Spite of Silence

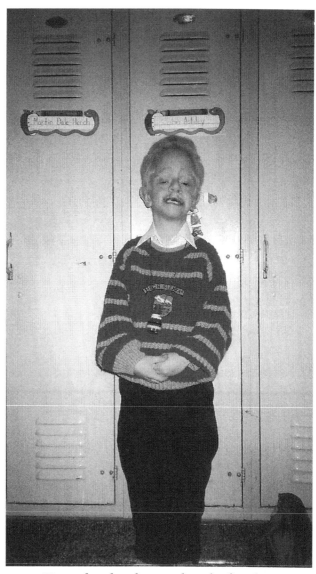

First day back to school after his
kidney transplant

Finally in the hearing-impaired program!

Johnny in 7th grade, he always put his
pencil behind his ear

Chapter Eight

Rest In Spite of the Labor

Matthew 11:28-29 "Come unto me, all ye that labor and are heavy laden, and I will give you rest. Take my yoke upon you, and learn of me; for I am meek and lowly in heart: and ye shall find rest unto your souls."

Being a caregiver can be very exhausting. The stress that is in the day-to-day takes a heavy toll. Most of the time as you care for a loved one you don't realize how much stress you are under. That can be very dangerous for the caregiver. We must be aware that caring for another's needs most of the time means that we don't care for our own needs.

The body and the mind need rest. God didn't design us to work like a machine. When we are over-stressed though, like a machine, we will break down. It's not a matter of if, but when it will happen. It may not be a major breakdown, but there will come a time that maintenance must be done. It may come in the form of sleep, getting a "brain break", or finding some time for yourself.

In Spite Of

Whenever Johnny was going to be in the hospital for an extended period of time, Joann and I would take turns spending the night in his room "sleeping" in a chair next to his bed. Some nights we would both end up staying the night if there was a serious problem with Johnny's health. The point is that we learned through the years that just being in a hospital is tiring. Most of the days are spent just waiting-waiting for the doctors to round, waiting for a test, waiting for the nurse to bring medications, waiting for the dinner tray. The waiting is endless and exhausting. There is also the stress of wondering what might happen next. The need for rest is great.

We would co-ordinate our schedules between Joann's job and the church business that I needed to attend to and make sure that one of us would go home at night to get some real sleep in our own bed and a shower so that we could feel human the next day. This worked pretty well for us. The value of a good night of sleep cannot be over emphasized. If you are a caregiver, you need to get your rest!

There were times that Johnny's condition was severe and we would both stay the night in order to be a comfort to one another in case something went wrong. Sometimes there were days of no sleep and a lot of stress. Those were times when we could only look heavenward for the rest that can only come from the Lord. As we would count on Him to take care of our son, we would have to depend upon His care for us.

As Johnny and his brothers got older we were able to leave the house for a "date night." Joann and I would get an evening to go out for dinner together. This was a wonderful treat for us. A little respite from caregiving and some time for us. We were always so grateful that Johnny's brothers were willing to care for him and give us a break.

When our sons Bob and Jason went off to college and were not available to help care for their brother, there was one woman that was a particular blessing to Joann and me. She was a member of our deaf church, she was hearing, but spent most of her time in our services for the deaf. She had her own set of health needs that caused her to be on oxygen all the time. She volunteered to watch Johnny for us so that we could go to church together on Wednesday nights. This was such a blessing for us, because we knew that Johnny was in good hands and she could communicate with him.

Eventually the Lord took her home to heaven, however, we were very grateful that she was willing to spend that time caring for Johnny. We all really missed her when she went to her heavenly home, but she and Johnny have been reunited.

The advice I always give to anyone that will listen is when you have a loved one in the hospital, get your rest when you can. You will need to be your best when they are discharged from the hospital and go home. If you allow yourself to get run down then you won't be any good to the one you want to care for. As a caregiver you generally put yourself last to care for the needs of your loved one. Just be aware that getting rest is the best thing you can do for yourself and in turn for the ones that you care for.

I remember a hospitalization that Johnny had that was about two weeks long. Joann and I tried to keep a good schedule of getting rest and it seemed like it worked well. This stay was a particularly difficult one, we almost lost him one night, which was followed by several days in intensive care. We finally were discharged on my birthday and we were all worn out. When we got home my back was bothering me (that can happen from sleeping in those hospital chairs) so I got down on the living room floor to stretch my back. I don't remember if I ever stretched or not; I just remember waking up about three hours later stiff and sore from sleeping on the floor. I definitely felt my age that night.

In Spite Of

One night several years ago, Johnny was admitted with pulmonary edema. His oxygen saturation was low, but he seemed stable. It was my turn to go home and man was I looking forward to it! The forecast was for a snow storm to come through that night and Joann said that she thought I should spend the night at the hospital. Being the stubborn man that I am and the fact that I had a hot shower on my mind, I told her I was going to go home and the snow storm wouldn't affect me.

Well, I left, going against the advice of my wife (and her mother's intuition)-a decision I would later regret (I hate it when that happens). The snow was coming down pretty hard when I left the hospital. I made it home and got that hot shower and settled in for a long winter's nap, or so I thought. About 2:30am the phone rings and it's Joann. Johnny had gotten worse overnight and he was in some distress and they suggested that I come to the hospital.

By now there was about ten inches of snow on the ground and it was still coming down heavily (why didn't I listen to her?) I told her I was on my way. There was no traffic out (go figure) and I was just guessing where the road was for most of the forty-five mile trip. On the freeway at least there were reflectors on the side so I had some idea of where the road was. Having a death grip on the steering wheel I traveled about twenty five miles an hour. Finally a truck passed me and forged a way for me to follow. After about two hours I arrived back at the hospital. Joann didn't say "I told you so" that night, nor did she need to. Some things are just better left unsaid.

Once when Johnny was in critical, but stable, condition in the hospital while he was in intensive care, his brothers wanted to see him and give us a break from spending the night in his room. They were both living in Atlanta, Georgia at the time. So our oldest son, Bob, left his wife Rebekah and children in Georgia and he, Jason, and Jason's wife Kristin drove all day to get to Michigan (a twelve hour drive) to relieve Joann and me. Our sons were worried about their brother for sure, but also knew the toll that being in the hospital took on mom and dad. That was such a blessing for us, especially when you consider that they left the next morning and drove all day back to Atlanta.

As a caregiver the word "rest" many times is a dream we have. Caring for another person will take away your energy and there is often no hope of relief. That is when we looked to the Lord to give us the strength and wisdom we needed to make good decisions for Johnny's care. Trusting in the Lord was the only constant in our lives. He strengthened us day by day and gave us rest and peace in spite of it all.

Isaiah 40:31 " But they that wait upon the Lord shall renew their strength; they shall mount up with wings as eagles; they shall run, and not be weary; and they shall walk, and not faint."

2 Corinthians 4:16 " For which cause we faint not; but though our outward man perish, yet the inward man is renewed day by day."

In Spite Of

Chapter Nine

Coping In Spite of Pressure

Ecclesiastes 9:10 "Whatsoever thy hand findeth to do, do it with thy might; for there is no work, nor device, nor knowledge, nor wisdom, in the grave, whither thou goest."

Johnny was a very creative and artistic person. With his physical limitations he couldn't entertain himself playing sports or running around outside. He spent much of his time working on "projects" I guess you would call them. These were no ordinary art projects that he would create. They were in many ways his way of working through the frustrations of being trapped in a body that just didn't work right.

At a young age he began working through many of his medical procedures by performing them on his stuffed animals. He had a stuffed Mickey Mouse that he did many different surgeries on. Everything from a "G" tube to a kidney transplant, poor Mickey would get cut open and sewed back together after Johnny had recovered from his own procedures. Johnny would even give Mickey enemas that he would make out of paper and tape. Mickey had a set of leg braces and scars all over his body.

In Spite Of

Johnny's medical procedures were not exclusive to poor Mickey though, we found a stuffed dinosaur in our basement, shortly after Johnny's passing, that he had been working on also. Dino had a tracheotomy and a bandage on his chest (heart surgery we assume) along with a fill stem from a beach ball that he sewed on the dinosaur for a "G" tube.

Johnny had a talent for creating things from paper and tape. He would spend countless hours in his room building his creations. We would buy reams of paper and rolls of tape on a consistent basis.

His projects varied from small things such as a working tape measure to, much bigger creations, like a building that was being built that was on his route to school each day. As the building would go up Johnny would replicate each step in the process. He re-created the building on a large piece of cardboard and started with the frame and continued to the finished building. This included flooring and office furniture.

Some of his buildings required special trips so he could look inside them to insure he was making his buildings realistic. He had a particular fascination with abandoned buildings. One such building wasn't too far from our home. It was an old house on a busy road and he would always try to get me to stop so he could look in the windows to finish the interior of the home. I never wanted to stop because it was a vacant home and it was on a very busy street with very little room to park. Well, one day Johnny's persistence finally got to me and I stopped reluctantly to have a look inside.

I helped Johnny up the old porch steps and he was able to look in the front windows. He was delighted to see the inside of an old vacant house. I had to pick him up so he could look in some windows on the side of the house. With the mission accomplished, I headed down the front porch steps to return to the car. It was a cold and rainy fall day and as I took my first step down the stairs my feet slipped out from under me and down the steps I went on my backside bouncing down each step. Did I mention this house was on a very busy street? Humiliated and bruised, I turned to help Johnny down the steps and to the car. He never asked to go see that house again.

One of the projects that Johnny was most proud of was a six-pack of hard lemonade he had created out of paper and tape. He really liked the logo on the bottles and the case they came in. He never drank it nor was it ever in the house. He just picked it up from the commercials on the television. One of our neighbors that just loved Johnny was visiting one day and Johnny was proudly showing her his newest projects he was working on. She fell in love with his six-pack and wanted to buy it from him. He wasn't interested in letting go of it at all. She kept raising the price and got to $20.00, but Johnny said, "No this is mine and you can't have it." She finally gave up in disbelief.

Johnny's creations were his unless he made them as a gift. He took great pride in his work and had no interest in parting with any of his projects.

One Fourth of July he had put together boxes of fireworks that he had made out of paper and tape. He assembled these based on an advertisement that had come in the mail for mail-order fireworks. The detail that he could put into his projects was amazing. The fireworks were for display only of course, however his brother Jason talked him into letting him light off one of the rockets he had made. Without Johnny knowing Jason had put a real rocket inside Johnny's paper one, Jason lit the paper on fire and Johnny watched half laughing at his brother, "This isn't going to work. It's only paper and..." suddenly the rocket inside ignited and tried to lift off the ground. It didn't go very far, but for a split second Johnny believed he was better at building fireworks than he thought.

In Spite Of

Johnny's creativity didn't stop with paper and tape. He also loved to draw. Many times he worked through his hospital stays and surgeries by making story boards of what had happened to him while in the hospital. His stories would contain all the places he would go and the people he would see. His interpreters would have to go into the operating room with him many times until he would be put under anesthesia. They would always comment on how Johnny would be looking around and absorbing everything he could before falling asleep.

Fashion was also one of Johnny's interests. He had a different taste in clothing than his parents would have liked him to have, but that was Johnny. He was unique in so many ways. He really liked the whole Gothic thing. He would try to purchase clothing along those lines and became very frustrated because all the clothes that he liked were too big for him. Not willing to accept the fact that he couldn't buy the clothing he liked, he began making his own clothes!

He would buy black jeans and some black denim material and make his baggie pants. He took paperclips and pop can tabs to make chains and buttons. Once again, he would be in his room for hours working on his clothing. Then he would proudly wear the clothes to school showing off all his hard work. He made hooded sweatshirts and would draw designs on countless T-shirts. He truly was a fashion buff.

Many of the clothes he made were for other people. He would give them as gifts to those that were close to him. They may never wear them in a public place, but they will be forever treasured possessions to each person that received them.

One of the T-shirts that Johnny made was also a bit of therapy for him. After he had his second heart valve replaced, he spent a few days in intensive care. His recovery was going very well and it looked like he might be moved to a room in the main hospital sooner than expected. Then one night the nurse that was taking care of him gave him a very strong sedative that really set his recovery back. He slept most of the next day and was "loopy" when he was awake. After he got home from the hospital he designed a T-shirt with a picture of a mean looking nurse with a big syringe in her hand, with the caption, "Where's the nurse that made me dizzy?" on it.

A large portion of our basement is dedicated to storing many of Johnny's creations. There are plastic bins full of books, boxes with his buildings and six packs. They all represent his creativity and genius to us as well as countless hours of work, reams of paper, and rolls of tape. During his life these works of art were precious to him and he was never willing to give them up. Now, they belong to us. All these projects are just as precious to his family today as they were to Johnny and now we don't want to let them go either.

Johnny learned to cope with his many trials by keeping his mind and hands busy in making his creations. When he didn't have a project he was working on, he would quickly become bored and would get discouraged about his limitations. Keeping ourselves busy is a good way to help us from being discouraged by our "In Spite Of" situations.

Chapter Ten

Inspiration In Spite of it All

1 Corinthians 1:2 "But God hath chosen the foolish things of the world to confound the wise; and God hath chosen the weak things of the world to confound the things which are mighty;"

When Johnny was eight years old we took a trip to visit my mom in Florida once again. Only this time we had to travel via North Carolina to pick up our other sons from camp. After retrieving them we continued south and spent the night in St. Augustine in north Florida on the Atlantic coast. It is a very beautiful city and we enjoyed our time there. We spent as much time as we could on the beach before traveling on to see Mom.

While on the beach Johnny decided he wanted to build a sand castle. I was in the ocean with Bob and Jason, mom was relaxing on a blanket we had brought. I was watching Johnny from the distance as he struggled to take a bucket and carefully walk across the sand to an area of the beach that he could get some wet sand, maybe twenty yards from the blanket. This may sound like an easy task to most, but for Johnny it was a very hard trek.

In Spite Of

The reason being Johnny didn't walk till he was almost five years old and most of the time he wore leg braces to support him. Now, on the beach, he was without the braces and on the uneven sands and without anything to hold on to made the journey precarious.

With bucket in hand and both arms out for balance, Johnny headed off to build his castle. When he arrived at the place where he would make his new creation, he realized that he had forgotten the plastic shovel he would need to dig in the sand. As I watched from the water I could see the wheels spinning in his head, "Do I go back to get the shovel? Do I try to get Mom's attention? Or do I just make due with what I have? After all, the walk will be hard to navigate there and back again."

I watched and tears filled my eyes as he dropped the bucket and headed back to the blanket. Each step was taken with caution, but with great determination. (To the blanket and back to the construction site.) The short walk for us was a monumental task for him. However, he made the trip without complaining or asking for any help. Finally having everything he needed for building his castle he got to work, satisfied in his quiet world, just him, the bucket, and the shovel.

This may not sound like much of an inspirational story to most, but for me it was a huge moment. At that moment in my life I decided that as best I could I would not allow myself to ever give up! No matter how hard life would get, I would remember that moment and allow it to be my motivation when things got tough. I was the only witness to what happened that day on the beach and I believe it was meant just for my eyes. I am so grateful that I was witness to the strength of a king going to build his castle.

Although I was the only one that saw Johnny's determination that day, I would relay that moment to my wife and our other two sons. I remember telling Bob and Jason, "If we could put Johnny's determination in their healthy bodies, that nothing would be able to stop you." Then again, it may have been Johnny's weak body that gave him that determination. The strong spirit that God gave Johnny rubbed off on all of us through the years.

Johnny's influence went far beyond our immediate family though. One of Joann's cousins told us that her husband has a picture of Johnny on the bulletin board above his desk in his home office. One day Lisa walked into the office and spotted the picture and said, "That's really nice that you have Johnny's picture to look at." He replied, "Do you know why I have that picture there?" She thought it was just a memorial of sorts. He said, "When I'm having a bad day, I look at Johnny's picture to remind myself, that no matter how bad my day is, it is still better than his best days."

Johnny was what I liked to call a "perspective check" for people. When we think we have things bad, we always need to remember there are plenty of people that have troubles and problems far worse than ours. I always tell people when they have problems that they need to go down to the children's hospital and just sit in the emergency room or go to the intensive care area and just listen to what others are dealing with to get new perspective on their situation.

When Johnny was fifteen years old he began attending Michigan School for the Deaf in Flint, Michigan. This was a great move for him and he flourished there. Many of the teachers there were deaf themselves and were good role models for him and all the students there. The hearing faculty all knew sign language and Johnny's communication skills really improved. Those were good years for him there.

The time finally came for Johnny to graduate from school. This was a day that we weren't sure would ever come, and now we were preparing for all the festivities that go along with graduation.

In Spite Of

This, however, would be one of the grandest moments of Johnny's and his parents' lives.

Two of Johnny's teachers at school were very moved by his ever present smile and good attitude. Even when he was tired and sick, he usually had a smile on his face and would brighten up their day. Because of that they decided to establish an award in Johnny's honor and called it the "John Ashley Inspiration Award". This award was presented to Johnny at his commencement ceremony. Needless to say, his mom and dad were very proud and overwhelmed with emotions as he received the award.

Seated on the platform that day was the superintendent of schools for the state of Michigan, Mike Flanagan. He was so moved by Johnny's story and his strength that he and his wife established a scholarship award to be given each year at MSD. This past June Joann and I were able to give out Johnny's Inspiration award to the graduate that, in spite of adversity, kept a good attitude and overall sunny disposition. Mr. Flanagan was there to present his scholarship award to a student and he told us that it was Johnny that prompted him and his wife to establish their award.

When Johnny was maybe five or six years old, I would pray that God would use him in a special way someday. This was my prayer every morning for much of a year until one morning as I prayed, God spoke to my heart as plain as day, and said, "I am using him right now." From that day forward I never prayed that way again. I could only observe the power God showed through his life.

Having Johnny in our family took us on a course we certainly would have never chosen on our own. However, I would not trade it for another life. A verse of Scripture that I have loved and prayed since I have become a "seasoned citizen" is Psalm 71:18 *"Now also when I am old and greyheaded, O God, forsake me not; until I have shewed thy strength unto this generation, and thy power to every one that is to come."* My desire has been that those that have faith in Christ would go beyond just a casual relationship and into a deep trusting relationship with Christ. I desire to be an example of His power and strength.

The thought that I always had was that God would do some great work in my life or in our church that would inspire the next generation to trust God. After Johnny's passing this verse spoke loud and clear to me. For twenty-eight years God's strength and power has been on display through Johnny's life and the testimony of our family. Not that we are anything special, but the God we served through all these years has poured out His strength and power upon us all. He heard my prayer from the locker room in the hospital the day Johnny was born as I begged Him, through my tears, for grace and strength.

It was the inner strength that Johnny possessed that has inspired so many, and he has left an unforgettable mark on countless lives. Through all his surgeries and medical procedures through the years, he rarely complained. There were times that he would be in a dental chair for up to four hours and would still entertain the dentist and his aides. I was always in awe of how strong his spirit was.

Johnny inspired the world that he could reach with his life. I believe that we all should have a hope in our hearts that we could have an impact on other people as we live our everyday lives. His memorial service was a bittersweet event. We were rejoicing for Johnny that his struggles had come to an end, but we sorrowed for the loss of such an inspiration.

I would like to share some of the comments that people have made on social media or through the emails we received about the impact Johnny had on their lives.

In Spite Of

His oldest brother Bob wrote "If you knew him, he melted your heart. My Heart is breaking having to say goodbye too soon. My brother and my hero is resting in heaven tonight. Nothing holding him back any longer."

His brother Jason wrote "If you knew him, he changed your life. Enjoy heaven my brother and best friend. You deserve it more than anyone I know"

John Harwell, a friend of both Jason and Bob said "Johnny made everybody better. He taught us all lessons about life that I think we are still learning. He was courageous, brilliant, and loyal. Bob and Jason, you guys were great brothers to him. I've always looked up to all 3 of you. Rest assured he's receiving crowns in heaven."

Pat Chillik, one of Johnny's teachers from Michigan School for the Deaf wrote "John....smiling....and artist....friendly.... inspiring....So many words can describe the young man I saw as my student at MSD! I'm sure he was welcomed into the Pearly Gates by a multitude!! I know I always looked forward to having him in my classes! All those wonderful memories YOU have will keep John with you 'til eternity when you shall meet again! Until then....you have an Angel watching over you....John is certainly one! Your faith will keep you strong as another chapter of your life unfolds and the little Miracle Nixon, gets to know and love you! God's plans are amazing! Thank God we believe!"

Dave Roddy, a former police officer and member of our church said "You were more than a hero to so many, Johnny. Your life defined courage, strength, perseverance, love and faith. We are sad in losing you but are comforted and rejoice in knowing you are in the arms of Jesus. "Cya later buddy" ...Dave

Christa Moran, one of Johnny's interpreters from the University of Michigan Hospital "We all did indeed love John. I have been fortunate enough over these past 10 years to know , laugh with , read his books, hear his stories and watch what an incredible and strong person he is. It has been a privilege and honor to work with you. He and you as a family have taught me many lessons that I will carry with me always. I will miss him and his beautiful smile.

Trisha Mazariegos, Our former Pastor's daughter and someone who grew up with Johnny being part of her life, upon hearing of Johnny's death "I'd like to just let you know that I love you and your family. Your constant testimony of grace under fire has been lived out daily, monthly... Yearly... All of Johnny's life, in fact, for all those who've been privileged to be near you. I'm so grateful that God allowed me to see your faith in action for so much of my childhood and throughout the in-between years. There've been several occasions when I've thought, 'If the Ashley's can remain faithful and true to God in less-than-ideal situations and times of life, I need never even contemplate doubting God or His plan in my down moments of life.'"

As I have already mentioned, there have been many great medical professionals that have cared for our son. Through the years we have gotten close to many of them. There is however, two of Johnny's heart doctors that we grew particularly close to at the U of M hospital. I asked if they would be willing to write about their experience of caring for Johnny and allow me to include their comments in this book. They were both more than happy to share their thoughts.

Doctor Gregory Ensing is a Clinical Professor of Pediatrics and Pediatric Cartiology at the University of Michigan School of Medicine and was Johnny's cardiologist for eleven years. He wrote:

With love, respect and admiration for John Ashley
In 2005 , I received a call from my good friend and colleague, Rick Humes, who asked that I begin to follow one of his patients, a 17 year

In Spite Of

old young man who had already undergone 2 major heart operations, a kidney transplant, four additional operations, and who was moving to our area. Dr. Humes described John as "unusual looking", deaf, and unable to speak. He added, "you may at first think he is kind of slow but please don't underestimate him. He is one of my favorites." Finally, Dr. Humes mentioned that John Ashley was in need of a third heart operation, this time to replace another heart valve. Thus began my most unique and one of my most cherished relationships.

The next week I saw John with his mother, a signing translator, and his pastor father. John was ill. As I examined this seemingly frail young man, I could not help but think of the hundreds of prayers his parents must have shared and wonder how many seemed to go unanswered. In short order, we replaced John's mitral valve with minimal damage to his transplanted kidney. John recovered amazingly quickly and was soon home.

John and his parents, signing translator in tow, returned for visits several times each year. Many times John was doing well. More often, his health was a little worse—either worsening heart function, a transplanted kidney that was sliding, more narrowing of his spine limiting his ability to walk, or a nasty infection. Still, each time I was greeted with bright twinkling eyes, an infectious smile and a snarky translated greeting. Without speaking, John flirted with every nurse, and charmed every resident, fellow and medical student. Each visit's goodbye was with an appreciative smile and a warm hug. On the good days, but also on the worst, John without speaking made each of us feel better about ourselves and about the world around us. Somehow he cared for us even more than we cared for him. In 2016, after several more surgeries and hospitalizations, John's kidney failed and he made the decision that the long struggle had reached its end.

Since that time, I learned that this disabled young man inspired his teachers, his classmates, his translators, and nearly everyone he encountered in the same way he affected me. John's warmth, his love for his family, and his enthusiasm for life were communicated in a way that words would never have sufficed. John, his loving mother, and his pastor father made the world a better place for all they met. I thank God for this one of a kind young man and for the special way that he changed us all.

Doctor Mark Norris is an Adult Congenital Heart, Pediatric Cardiologist, and Assistant Professor University of Michigan School of Medicine. He took over Johnny's cardiac care when he was transferred from pediatric to adult cardiology. He wrote:

It is the exception not the rule for a pediatric cardiologist to seek me out to speak in person about an individual under their care who is ready to change from pediatric to adult heart care. Usually this passing of the baton, this graduation from the pediatric heart clinic, is done by a letter or email containing an abbreviated medical summary and plan. Instead, I first learned of John Ashley from an earnest pediatric cardiologist who pulled me aside to convey John's story and to secure my dedication to his ongoing care. So it was with great interest that I met with John for the first time as he was recovering from a hospitalization.

As a clinician, my observation of John began at the opening of the door. His body proportions spoke to atypical bone growth, his cleft lip to early surgeries, his leg braces to unclear strength and mobility. His eye contact was focused, warm, inquiring. I remember looking at each other during this first and many conversations that followed. John's thoughts put into sign were transposed to speech for me by his mother most often and sometimes his father. His mother who had greeted me a minute before, began to speak to me for him in a voice I came to recognize as distinctively John's. It is this voice that I hear in recalled conversations with John, the tenor and timber that were his. In this voice matched to a face so ready to break into a smile I learned of his humor and wit. In this same voice I understood in part John's deep desire to be healthy and to live life without the constraints of scheduled dialysis and doctors visits. His accomplishments and impact to that point were astounding, and he had plans for more. John was outsized for the physical body I found him in that day. The devotion of his parents was palpable, and John was buoyed by his ability to help others. Family photos hinted at the impact and the investment of past teachers in John's life. Still, this discrepancy between the man and his condition were not easily reconciled, and it was in this contrast that the distinction was made so clear. John was not leg braces and a curve of the back. And in spite of the time and attention to his internal anatomy and function, he was not a patched heart or a scarred kidney. It was not my medical acumen that elevated attention to these things; it was John.

John gifted me with a deep and meaningful conversation several years later. Medical problems were not going well, and John was back in the hospital. Although he quickly recovered and returned home, the prospect of progressive illness was real. He and I were again discussing the limitations of the medical options before him. John interjected and dismantled the calculus of my medical reasoning and risk assessments. From John's vantage point, he saw the path forward more clearly than I could. Looking over and beyond these struggles he said, "I want to be with Jesus. No pain. No tears. Right? We all want that." John was outsized for the physical

In the last few years of Johnny's life his pain became constant and more intense. He used a walker to get around most of the time because he never fully recovered from a surgery he had on his spine. We watched him slowly become weaker and talk more about how he hurt daily. One night as he was preparing for bed and his mom and he were about to pray, he asked his mom if it would be all right if he didn't kneel beside his bed to pray because it hurt so much. His mother, through her tears, said, "Of course it will be all right, God will hear your prayers if you just sit on the bed." He was always concerned that he would be doing the right thing.

Being an inspiration to others was never a goal nor a reality to Johnny. He merely lived his life as best he could with the limitations he had. He had no idea how much he impacted the lives of those around him. Whether you knew him for a moment or over many years, he really had an influence on how you looked at life.

Graduation Day, June 2008
Johnny receiving the "John Ashley Inspiration Award"

Proud parents of their "Silent Hero"

Chapter Eleven

Joy In Spite of Grief

Psalm 116:15 "Precious in the sight of the Lord is the death of his saints."

For the last two years of Johnny's life he was on kidney dialysis three times a week. The transplant that he had at the age of ten finally failed after seventeen years. As I have already mentioned, the average life of a transplant from a non-related donor is five to ten years. God had given Johnny's transplant a longer- than-expected life.

When Johnny's kidney finally failed, his health really began to go downhill. He became weaker as time went on and the dialysis treatments were hard on him. He also endured three line infections in the catheter that was used for dialysis.

The hardest thing for us to watch was when Johnny lost his plans for the future. He became more and more despondent as time went on. He had planned to get married and have an apartment at one time; he wanted no children or pets, but he had plans for his future. His qualifications for a wife were very high. Then he came to realize that his health was probably as good as it would ever get. So he just gave up on his plans.

In Spite Of

We can only imagine the pain that he suffered from daily. This too wore on Johnny. The doctors tried different medications to give him some relief, but for the most part they really didn't help. The side effects of some were too drastic for Johnny to handle; he didn't like the way they made him feel so he wouldn't take them.

After about a year of dealing with dialysis and the pain, he decided he had had enough. He began to talk of wanting to just go to heaven. For the first time in Johnny's life he had lost his will to fight. This too was difficult for us to see happen to him. He was always such a fighter; that's what got him through all the surgeries and hospital stays through his twenty-eight years. Now he had lost hope for his future and it broke his family's heart, but, we understood.

This led Johnny to have some very frank discussions with his family and his doctors. He made his own advanced directive up for the dialysis center and the hospital. He knew that he didn't want anyone to bring him back to life if he died, no CPR, no tracheotomy, no extraordinary efforts to keep him alive. He was listed at the hospital as "Do Not Resuscitate" or DNR. Most of his specialists understood, but many of the doctors on the kidney transplant floor didn't understand why a twenty-eight year old would want to give up on life.

There was one doctor in particular that probably wasn't much older than Johnny himself that questioned me about it. I told him that this was his decision and that the medical field could bring him back to life, but they couldn't give him a healthy body. He would still be in pain, wear leg braces, be on dialysis and not be able to hear. He was unwilling to agree with Johnny's choice, but he respected it.

Johnny began setting dates for his departure. First it was going to be in the fall of 2014, then the spring of 2015. That changed because he wanted to go to a Tiger baseball game that summer, so then it was August. You see Johnny told us he wanted to quit dialysis and let nature take its course. He was very matter-of-fact about that and was well aware of the fact that he would die if he did indeed give up dialysis.

Let me pause and say that the people that work in dialysis suites have a very difficult job. We are so grateful to those that worked with Johnny. They took such good care of him and really loved him. Every time Johnny came into the center he made a grand entrance. Everyone there knew when Johnny showed up. Those doctors, nurses and techs see people at their worst for the most part. People are sick, many get cramps while they are having their treatments, and they have to keep being professional and do their jobs under hard circumstances. We thank the Lord for the folks that do the work in the dialysis centers across this country.

There was one doctor that had to have some of the more difficult conversations with Johnny about his desire to give up on life. We all sat in his office as Johnny (through the interpreter) told the doctor of his plans to stop dialysis because his pain was so great. As we were all fighting back tears the doctor said that what Johnny was talking about needed to be handled by a palliative care doctor. They would have access to medications and resources that he didn't have knowledge of. So he referred us to a new doctor of palliative care. Not only could he deal with Johnny's desires, but could also be more aggressive in pain management.

The palliative care doctor was very kind and compassionate. He spent a lot of time with us discussing the process and trying to manage Johnny's pain. These appointments with him were very surreal. The conversations were blunt and open-a hard thing to do when you're talking about your son. One thing he requested was that we go and visit a psychiatrist to have an evaluation of Johnny's mental state so there would be no objections by other professionals to his choices.

In Spite Of

We went to visit this psychiatrist shortly thereafter. The doctor seemed pleasant enough and asked Johnny why he was there. Again through the interpreter Johnny explained all the reasons he wanted to stop dialysis and go to heaven. The doctor called his idea of heaven "fantasy thinking" and that such thoughts were an encouragement for him to want to die.

Joann about came unglued! This doctor was attacking the very faith that she had been talking to Johnny about for the last two years. Joann and Johnny would spend many evenings alone while I would be out doing church business. Johnny's faith was in God and he was confident of heaven and he would ask his mom about what it would be like for him to arrive there. Joann would sit with him and tell him that he would not suffer in pain anymore and that he would be whole and have a healthy body. These conversations were so intimate and so precious to a mother who was watching her precious child live in pain and give up on his dreams. She was giving him hope for his future based on the Bible and her vivid imagination. And now this doctor was telling us that what we believe is a fantasy and that is why our son wanted to die.

I told the doctor that she was speaking to a Baptist pastor and his wife and that our faith is the foundation for our family. "But let's put faith aside," I said, "the pain that our son has endured for his whole life and the fact that he will never get any better is the reason he has had enough". The fantasy thinking, as she called it, is the hope that we have in a life after death and not a fairy tale.

The conversation ended without any arguments or heated debate and as we left she said, "I would like to meet with you again." Well, needless to say, that was the last time we met with her, although she did say Johnny was able to make a clear judgment concerning his decision to quit dialysis.

Watching your child suffer has to be one of the most difficult things to experience as a parent. Especially for twenty eight-years. Now please understand that for most of those years we had lots of fun and many good times. However, interspersed among those good times were many months of pain and suffering. And the last two were the worst. Most nights after dialysis Johnny would cry and just say he wanted to go to heaven.

Johnny began to pray that God would just take him home. He would tell us that when he would wake up and realize he was still alive he would be disappointed. His way of checking to see if he had died in the night was to feel for teeth with his tongue. When he would feel the empty space from his cleft he knew he hadn't gotten the new body he so looked forward to. Many times he would say, "Jesus is stubborn" because He hadn't taken him to heaven.

The hardest decision Joann and I ever had to make was whether or not we would begin to agree with Johnny in prayer for God to give him relief and take him home. Mouthing those words were so difficult to do, but could we be selfish and ask God to keep him here to suffer longer? So, at his request, we began to pray with him and ask God to take Johnny home and free him from the pain he was in. Both of his brothers and many of our friends were also praying for Johnny to get his glorified body.

Had we known the pain we would feel when God answered our prayers, I don't know that I could have prayed that way. Our love for Johnny is so deep that our grief has been just as deep.

Johnny kept setting dates that he was going to quit dialysis and then cancelling them. Then on Saturday, October 3, 2015 God took that decision out of Johnny's hands.

Joann had left to fly to Atlanta to see our new grandson that was just two weeks old. Nixon decided to come five weeks early and surprise us all, so Grandma was excited to see that new baby. Johnny and I dropped Joann off at the airport and Johnny signed "I love you" to his mom for the last time. Then he and I headed off to dialysis.

After dialysis that day we ate out at Johnny's favorite restaurant (All the waitresses are pretty young girls) and went home for the evening. That night was pretty normal; we watched the Tigers on television and we went to bed.

That next morning I was up early as usual and Johnny was sleeping in his room. Joann and I were texting back and forth about the baby and what the plans for the day were. I heard Johnny stirring in his room as I was in my office preparing some things that I needed to take to the church. I remember thinking he needed to hurry up because I had to leave soon, but not before I got his breakfast ready. So I decided to take a shower; then he should be ready to eat and then I could leave.

After I got dressed I came out of my room expecting Johnny to be seated at the kitchen table like every other day, but his bedroom door was still shut. I remember thinking, "Come on Johnny; I've got to go, you need to get up." So I opened his door and he was lying on his floor behind his walker. He had gotten up, made his bed, gotten dressed, opened the blinds on his windows, and God took him to heaven. He was free at last!

The moment we always thought would come, came. We just never would have believed it would come at home like it did. However, if Johnny could have planned it, it was exactly what he wanted. He wasn't in a hospital, no suffering and gasping for breath, no IVs. He went home from his favorite place, his room. A sudden cardiac event was what they determined to be the cause of death. He was home before his body hit the floor.

Calling Joann and telling her that Johnny was gone was the hardest phone call I have ever had to make. I told her that I had some very bad news; she thought I would tell her about a relative or a friend that had passed away. When I told her that Johnny was gone she didn't believe me at first. I had to repeat myself and tell her how sorry I was to give her the news. As we talked I could hear the ambulance sirens coming and had to hang up. I am so thankful that she had Jason with her and that Jason had her with him. Jason called his brother Bob and told him what had happened. Bob was able to get to our house to be with me in just a few moments after Johnny's death.

The sorrow and grief that we all feel is because we miss Johnny so much, but I wouldn't want him to have to suffer another moment like he was. Today he is doing quite well according to the Word of God. Revelation 21:4 "And God shall wipe away all tears from their eyes; and there shall be no more death, neither sorrow, nor crying, neither shall there be any more pain: for the former things are passed away."

Johnny has a mouth full of teeth, a strong body, and can hear. I know that many doubt the existence of heaven, and some even doubt the existence of God, but I agree with my brother in the Lord, Job, when he says in Job 19:25 "For I know that my redeemer liveth, and that he shall stand at the latter day upon the earth:"

I know that on, October 3, 2015 that Johnny's arrival into heaven was precious in God's sight. The first thing Johnny saw was the Lord smiling and saying "Welcome home." And yes Johnny, He thinks you're precious.

First time Uncle with his nephew Ryan

Johnny's last Tigers game Summer 2015

Johnny and his mother

Johnny and his father

Conclusion

The Conclusion in Spite of So Much More to Say

It is our hope and prayer that all those that will read this book would; examine their own lives and consider a relationship with Jesus Christ. It is only through asking God to forgive our sins, and by accepting Christ, that we can have that relationship and have an eternal home in heaven.

For many years people have tried to encourage Joann and me to write a book about Johnny's life. My thought was that the last chapter hadn't been written yet and we really never thought much about writing the book. Shortly after Johnny's death it was as if the Lord spoke to me and said, "The final chapter has been written; it's time to write the book."

So in obedience to what I believe the Lord wanted us to do, we have tried to bring honor to Johnny's life and to the Lord who allowed us to be his parents for twenty-eight years.

We know that Johnny's story is not all that unusual. There are families all over the world that could tell very similar stories. Many families have weathered much more difficult circumstances than we have. We felt compelled to share our story with you and maybe give a voice to those other families that have and maybe still are struggling today.

We all live our lives In Spite of our circumstances-some in spite of pain, some in spite of sorrow, some in spite of financial difficulties. But In Spite of something that weighs us down and can keep us from living our lives to the fullest. Our In Spite of situations don't define who we are; but they help shape us into who God wants us to be.

Jesus told His disciples to pick up their crosses daily and follow Him. What He was basically saying was for them to serve Him In Spite of their own pain and heartache. By looking after the needs of others, our problems diminish. They don't go away, however, they will be less of a "cross" as we seek to carry other people's burdens.

I know I've said much about our faith as a family in this book. I want you to please understand that our faith isn't about religion; it's about a relationship with Jesus Christ. I can tell you by the authority of the Bible that Johnny is in heaven today, not because of all he suffered or because he was a good person, but because he trusted in the One who died for his sin.

John 14:1-6 *Let not your heart be troubled: ye believe in God, believe also in me. In my Father's house are many mansions: if it were not so, I would have told you. I go to prepare a place for you. And if I go and prepare a place for you, I will come again, and receive you unto myself; that where I am, there ye may be also. And whither I go ye know, and the way ye know. Thomas saith unto him, Lord, we know not whither thou goest; and how can we know the way? Jesus saith unto him, I am the way, the truth, and the life: no man cometh unto the Father, but by me.*

In Spite of So Much More to Say

When Jesus left the earth some 2,000 years ago he went to prepare a place for all those who would believe in him. Not for those that would be religious, but those that would ask God to forgive their sin and would trust Christ's death on the cross for payment for that sin and receive Jesus as their Savior. The confidence that we have that Johnny is in heaven is because he one day made that decision. Now we have faith that we will see him again because each family member has also made that same choice to trust Christ at one time or another in our lives.

Many people have an idea of how a person can be an inspiration in this world we live in. I hope this account of Johnny's life and the work that he did may challenge our thinking. It's not the great inventions or discoveries that inspire although they have had a great impact on lives. To be an inspiration in today's world is to have a life well lived In Spite of. Johnny had such a life. May he continue to inspire many people through this book.

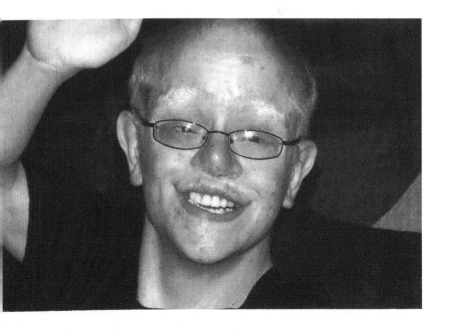

About the Authors

John & Joann Ashley

Pastor Ashley and Joann have co-authored the book *IN SPITE OF: The Johnny Ashley Story*. A book written about their son, Johnny's life and the inspiration he was to countless people. The book is also a testimony of how the Lord has sustained their family through the many years of having their faith consistently put to the test.

It is their firm belief that God gave them their son Johnny, and His strength so that they can use what the Lord has taught them to be a help to others. Everyone has an "In Spite Of" in their lives; some big, some small in comparison, but each one is real to those experiencing them.

With great passion and compassion, Pastor Ashley will encourage and challenge those in his audience to see their "In Spite Of" in a different light; not as a problem that God has allowed into their lives, but as an opportunity to see God's power in operation personally. Pastor Ashley is available to speak in churches, conferences, seminars, workshops and where ever there are people that are hurting.

In Spite Of

John and Joann have a special place in their hearts for caregivers. They know firsthand many of the challenges they face and desire to be a help and encouragement to them.

Pastor Ashley is currently traveling and preaching and sharing Johnny's story with his new endeavor, IN SPITE OF Ministries. His contact information as well as scheduling and recent articles can be found at livinginspiteof.com

IN SPITE OF ministries is devoted to, Educating, Encouraging, and Equipping people to use their IN SPITE OF situations as a catalyst for serving Christ and helping others. Whether physical, emotional, or spiritual challenges, we all have an IN SPITE OF in our lives. Far too often we allow our circumstances to define who we are; when God wants us to see our trials as opportunities to experience His grace and strength. Our IN SPITE OF situations are designed to build us into the people God intends us to be, so that we can demonstrate His great love to the world.

LIVINGINSPITEOF.COM

BibleNation.org

Your source of Biblical thought online

Visit the newly redesigned BibleNation.org and discover a bold and compelling Biblical perspective on current events and cultural issues.

Expert-written articles and videos engage the national and global culture with Biblical thought on news and topics including:

Morality & Ethics | Religion | Media & Arts | Science | Economics

This great resource is now online with new content and features.

 New Articles
 Video Series
Article Submission
Expert Authors
BNS Store

Make BibleNation.org part of your regular online experience.

 BibleNationSociety
 @BibleNation
 BibleNation

OTHER TITLES FROM BIBLE NATION

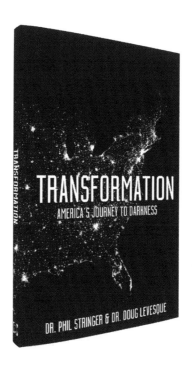

Transformation: America's Journey to Darkness

Dr. Phil Stringer & Dr. Doug Levesque

A civil war of values, of ideals, and of moral principles is occurring in America today. A Culture War for the future of American civilization is taking place. This war will be won or lost in your lifetime and the results of this war will be as significant as the results of the War for Independence. The war on life, law, family and freedom is being fought for dominance of American culture. Will the last vestiges of Christian culture be swept away? Or will there be a return to the foundations of this nation's Christian heritage? It is time for Christians to engage in the culture war that is transforming America.

Surviving This Babylon

Dr. Doug Levesque

Babylon never really died. Its pervasive influence fades and reappears like an unruly evil. Every mighty empire has been enticed by its attractive smile and ancient promises. America is no different. Inside such bait is always a hook. The United States is currently in the grips of "mystery, Babylon." Her lies are changing the heart and soul of this fine country. Good men and women are being deceived and drawn into perdition. Christians are suffering a modern day lions' den. The lions of Babylon are fierce but the ancient secrets revealed in Scripture will help you to roar back with a perfect boldness.

The Confident Shepherd

Dr. Doug Levesque

Sheep without a shepherd get fearful, scattered, sick and lost. Without a true and properly confident shepherd, the flock gets targeted by predators, stolen, and even killed. Shepherds are important to the general welfare and direction of society's flocks. It is possible to be a faithful shepherd. Multiple shepherds practicing the same skill set as the LORD Himself can turn society around.

Titles Available on Amazon.com

In Spite Of

In Spite Of

98261334R00080

Made in the USA
Columbia, SC
24 June 2018